THE JEWS
VIEWS AND COUNTERVIEWS

THE JEWS

VIEWS AND COUNTERVIEWS

A DIALOGUE

between

Jean Daniélou and André Chouraqui

NEWMAN PRESS

Westminster, Md. New York, N. Y. Glen Rock, N. J.

Amsterdam Toronto

Originally published as *Les Juifs* (cahier I de la revue VERSE ET CONTROVERSE) by Beauchesne Et Ses Fils, Paris, 1966. Original French edition 1966 by Beauchesne Et Ses Fils.

NIHIL OBSTAT:
William F. Hogan, S.T.D.
Censor Librorum

IMPRIMATUR:
✠ Thomas A. Boland, S.T.D.
Archbishop of Newark

April 18, 1967

Library of Congress
Catalog Card Number: 67-23607

Published by Newman Press
Editorial Office: 304 W. 58th St., N.Y., N.Y.   10019
Business Office: Westminster, Maryland   21157

Printed and bound in the
United States of America

Contents

5

Foreword

We know how much the Jewish question preoccupied the thoughts of numerous fathers of Vatican Council II, and how in particular the problem of anti-Semitism challenges the Christian conscience.

Going beyond the conciliar text on the Jewish problem, this book wishes to take bearings on the religious significance of Judaism, both for the Catholic and for the Jew, and also on the historic and human problem of anti-Semitism. An examination can indeed permit us to grasp more clearly the originality of Christianity in regard to its historic source, and to enter more fully into an understanding of the fact of the Jews as a permanent and inescapable question put to the conscience of Christians.

In order to penetrate into the heart of the matter, we have appealed to two eminent specialists who, in their concern for mutual charity, have not wished to remain silent on any difficulty, while limiting themselves to the essentials of the debate.

Father Daniélou, S.J., the present dean of the Faculty of Theology at the Catholic Institute of Paris, is one of the most important French theologians. A specialist in the history of Christian origins, he was one of the principal artisans of the renewal of biblical and patristic theology, and his numerous works devoted to this are now considered authoritative sources.

Far from isolating himself in purely theoretical research, Father Daniélou has shown himself to be one of the most active promoters of a living theology, concerned about its traditional sources and its responsibility in a world that poses urgent problems to Christian consideration.

A true missionary of the understanding of the faith and engaged particularly in the Jewish-Christian dialogue, Father Daniélou was clearly designated as the one to present with competence the Catholic point of view in the discussion presented in this book.

André Chouraqui was born in Ain-Témouchent, Algeria. After completing his secondary school work at the Lycée of Oran, he studied theology at the Rabbinical School of France, philosophy at the Sorbonne, and Oriental languages. A doctor of law and laureate of the Faculty of Law in Paris, he is a practicing lawyer in Oran.

From 1941 to 1945, he directed the network of resistance in Haute-Loire. Personal advisor to Ben-Gurion from 1959 to 1963, he became assistant mayor of Jerusalem in 1965.

As permanent delegate of the Universal Israelite Alliance, André Chouraqui has traveled and given lectures in Africa, America, Europe and the Near East.

CHOURAQUI—Throughout the last few decades, the American saying, "Jews are news," has unfortunately never ceased to prove its truth; the Jews have constantly nourished the current events of the last century. When one is a Jew, as I am, one can see the Judaic phenomenon from the inside, but though this is just as urgent as it appears to be, it never ceases to be a mystery.

A Jew, conscious of the event that informs him, has perhaps more than anyone else the feeling of moving in the midst of a paradox.

The essayists who have tried to explain the Jewish fact, such as Sartre or Memmi, have disclosed, above all, a negative fact. We can say that they use the apophatic method to define the existence of the Jew, not in relation to what he is but rather to what he is not.

Sartre in a very brilliant essay grants existence to the Jew in the measure that anti-Semitism condemns him. In this regard, Sartre explains much less the Jew, whom he does not know, than the anti-Semite who troubles him. With Sartre this point of view is clear and understandable; he belongs to the generation that has seen the rise and triumph of the horror of Hitlerism and the great massacres in concentration camps.

In Memmi such a view is more astonishing. He was born in Tunisia, in an environment where Judaism has its own reality, vitality and vigor. As a good disciple of Sartre, Memmi, in his *Portrait of the Jew,* explains the Judaic fact only in relation to its shadow, its negative counterpart. For him the Jew is a man considered in his absurd condition, imprisoned in an impasse.

This clinical explanation of the Jew in exile seems to constitute only a stage in the thought of Memmi. Like Camus and Sartre, Memmi is conscious of the absurdity of the human condition for which he seeks an outlet. He is now preparing a second essay on the Jews. Perhaps he will propose a positive solution to the Jews' condition, the absurdity and paradox of which he has already described for us. But will he succeed in this without introducing into his universe a transcendence without which, in my opinion, it is impossible to understand Israel?

When I compare the thought of Sartre and Memmi to my personal experience, I must say I scarcely recognize myself in the portrait they give of the Jew. On the contrary, what strikes me in the Jew's destiny is its irreducibly positive character. When I search in my memory, the anti-Semite is only a shadow that emanates from the Jew, not his essence. However cruel or absurd he has been toward me, I can say that he has never penetrated my being.

The most distant memory I have in this regard is the following. When I was still quite a small child, I was going with my father through a street of my native village to the synagogue of Ain-Temouchent in Algeria. An idler cried out some insult, probably calling us "dirty Jews." My father's reaction put the man to flight, to my great joy. My child's prayer that day undoubtedly must have been more fervent.

Thus the memories that force themselves upon me when I want to define what has made me a Jew are positive memories. I see again my father praying. Each morning at dawn he used to go to the synagogue where he put on his phylacteries and his prayer shawl; then he would read the Hebrew books and the bible, our Hebrew bible that had a place of honor in our home. There was the prayer at dawn, the afternoon and evening prayers to fill each day. In addition, my father constantly carried with him a psalm book that I have inherited; he used to read it every day. He knew his Hebrew psalms by heart. For him, to be a Jew was before all else to communicate in the inspiration of the bible and to pray in the fervent hope for the final accomplishments of man. Each of the doors of our house was ornamented with mezuzahs, nailed there in order to remind us of the biblical order of unity and love written in the language of the bible.

At my birth, prayers said in Hebrew and blessings taken from the bible welcomed me into this world. I know that at the age of eight days I was circumcised. To enter into the covenant of Abraham, I gave my blood so generously that I almost died from a hemorrhage. The anti-Semites, I must say, had no share of responsibility for this fact.

The Judaic option appears to me before all else as the free choice of a certain manner of being, inseparable from the biblical order known and respected in its original Hebrew versions. The progress of my existence has always been marked by this choice, and it was made according to the rhythm of biblical seasons. The three daily prayers, the Sabbath, the great biblical solemnities of the Passover, of Pentecost, of Tabernacles, of New Year's Day that celebrates the creation of the earth and heavens, or of the Great Atonement that prefigures the last judgment—such were the seasons and rites which distinguished the Jew. The Hebrew bible, read in its original tradition, constitutes for him the rock on which his being is founded.

Afterward, when I detached myself from myself in order to consider the fact of the Jew as a whole, I was confirmed in this intuition, and I saw the negative phenomenon, described by Memmi, only as secondary reality. Sartre can indeed say, "It is the anti-Semite who creates the Jew," but this explanation has value only in a world that has lost its sacred character and where the Jew himself is emptied of his substance; he does not know the liberty of choice that has imprinted a Jewish quality on his being.

As I have said, the history of Israel is made up of numerous paradoxes. One of them has the flavor of Jewish history: throughout the centuries the Jews have suffered martyrdom in order not to disappear. They have succeeded in surviving all persecutions, and now they are back in the Holy Land where they are rebuilding a new nation. Since the proclamation of the State of Israel, each one there is wondering what it means to be a Jew. The question is so important that a leader of the government, David Ben-Gurion, organized an international consultation. He asked the thinkers, the philosophers, the scholars and the rabbis of the entire world to tell him how to define a Jew. The answers given to this question are complex and often contradictory; in fact, this complexity and this contradiction are linked to the very essence of the Jew.

Catholicism and Islamism are both defined by relation to a concept, the first to the concept of universality, the second to one of submission to God. A Catholic is one who adheres to the creed of the Church; a Mohammedan is one who recites the *shahada* and shares in the intercession of the Prophet. The word *Judaism* has several meanings that show the complexity of the Jew's situation.

It is derived from a Greek root that means *to give thanks to God;* at its origin there was thus a reference to a definite spiritual attitude.

But the word serves to designate a country, Judea, as well as its inhabitants, the descendants of Juda, the Judeans, the Jews. There is a concrete reference to a spirituality, to a humanity and to a land; this, in my opinion, goes to the heart of the matter. This religion is characterized by the alliance of a God (the God of Sinai), of a people (Israel) and of a country (the Holy Land). The history of Judaism is that of the trinity which composes it. The message here is inseparable from the people who receive it, and the latter can be conceived only by the land where their accomplishments must be realized. The alliance is the more constraining as it is indissoluble. The infidelities of the people may drive them from their land and alienate them from their God, without annulling thereby the fact of their belonging both to heaven and to earth. Every contradiction introduced into the alliance of the word of eternity, with the man who has Israel for his name, and with the land where the message is to be realized, dissociates its living perfection.

Israel is essentially the hostage in a drama that dislocates the first unity, that of the heavens and the earth. The Jew then will never be able to find peace except in the harmony of the triad of which he is a part; hence the exceptional difficulty of avoiding misinterpretation and of defining exactly the perspectives of the revelation of Sinai. To speak only of the "permanent values" of Judaism or only of the wanderings of a people would be to falsify the situation that is characterized by the meeting of a God, a people and a land. An analyst, in sacrificing one of the fundamental components of the Judaic phenomenon, would misrepresent it.

In my eyes, one can be a Jew in a global manner in attaching oneself to the message, the people and the land of Israel. But one can also be a Jew in recognizing only one of them. In fact, each Jew chooses according to his liking the degree of fidelity that he intends to keep in regard to the message, the people and the land of Israel. The variations, one can say, are really innumerable. Today there are almost as many ways of being a Jew as there are Jews. This does not facilitate, of course, an understanding of what can be defined at the outset as the paradox, or, to use St. Paul's words, the mystery of Israel.

DANIÉLOU—The exposé that Mr. Chouraqui has just given interests me very much, in particular the last part where he distinguishes the different elements that, without being necessarily linked together, concur in constituting what is called a Jew. In listening to him, this is how things presented themselves to me—that is, from the point of view of Christians. I think that in what constitutes for us the Jewish problem, the different elements that Mr. Chouraqui distinguishes are not in reality on the same level; consequently they do not appear to us as forming a kind of bloc, even if this bloc cannot be, in a certain measure, dissociated.

In my opinion, it is an obvious fact—and Mr. Chouraqui has indicated it—that the term "Jew" corresponds to a certain ethnic category; in the extension of this category—for I believe that there is a close bond between the two—the term also corresponds to a certain land, that is, to a certain geographic reality.

CHOURAQUI—Allow me to interrupt you, Father. When I use the expression "Judaic ethnicity," I am far from making allusion to any form of racism whatever. I want to insist on this because the idea appears to me very important, particularly in Europe where the concept of a Jew has ended in designating exclusively a certain type of man. Often in Europe people say to me, "You do not look like a Jew." To convince these well-meaning souls of their error, I advise them to visit Israel. There one can see very well that there is no "Jewish type." There we find Jews who have come from 102 countries, from all the continents and from all types of civilization. It is sufficient to walk through the streets of Jerusalem, Tel-Aviv or Haifa to be clearly aware that no Jewish type exists. The only typology that stands out from this conglomeration, this assemblage of men who have come from all over the world, is the human type. You will find in Israel all types of men.

When I speak of ethnicity, it is not a question then of a physiological type such as can be defined at certain epochs here and there, but of a type attached to a cultural and historical tradition. I find it very striking that in the rest of the world the Jews for centuries have been considered by their fellow citizens as Jews; the Jew in Germany, in France, in England or in Mohammedan countries was only a Jew. Now that everyone has assembled in Israel, the common factor of Jewishness is annulled, and the Jew now is described in relation to the nation from which he came and which had always experienced almost unsurmountable difficulties in assimilating him. The German Jew in Israel is no longer a Jew but a German, the Moroccan Jew is no longer a Jew but a Moroccan, and so on.

DANIÉLOU—I think that there is some truth in what Mr. Chouraqui has said, but only up to a point. It is impossible to minimize, from the point of view of Jewish tradition itself, the idea of the descent from Abraham, which is something absolutely fundamental, and the idea of a certain ethnic community in the strict sense of the word, naturally implying intermixtures and without any racist character. But I am entirely in agreement with Mr. Chouraqui in saying that it is rather a question of a certain human type, that is to say, implying a cultural tradition with all it represents, and first of all from the linguistic point of view. Hebrew, which was the language of ancient Israel, constitutes, as does every other language, the expression of a certain structure of thought, and indisputably there is a bond between the fact of being a Jew and the fact of the Hebrew language. The bible is written in Hebrew and it is impossible to dissociate these two facts.

There is also the heritage of a certain culture represented, from the cultural point of view, by the ancient history of Israel in that admirable book which is the Old Testament. This, aside from the fact that we Christians also consider it an inspired book, is an extraordinary and incomparable work even if considered solely from the viewpoint of the typical genius it expresses.

Therefore, I think that we can observe here a certain tradition that makes Israel a people among the peoples of the world, and this is for me an essential point. Just as there are cultural traditions of China or of India, just as there is a cultural tradition belonging to Greece with its own language and an entire cultural heritage, so there is first a Jewish tradition that represents a certain human type and gives to this expression of a human type its highest significance: that is to say, in not reducing it entirely to one or another of its characteristics, but in giving it its whole signification.

From this point of view, Israel at first appears to an outsider as a people among the peoples of the world, and in this sense the land is linked to this problem. Never has it entered anyone's mind that the Christians should claim a country; Christians are not linked to any land. On the other hand, it seems to us wholly normal that Israel desires to be a nation among nations, and we even think that from this point of view the State of Israel has a remarkable significance precisely because it restores Israel to the assembly of peoples as a people having the right to be a people among peoples.

This appears to me to be of capital importance in indicating a radical distinction from what a Christian is. The Christian is absolutely not linked to any particular race, any human type or any country. Moreover, this is why it is quite normal to use an expression such as Judaeo-Christian to designate one who, from the standpoint of human types, is perfectly a Jew, but who at the same time, from the standpoint of religious adherence, is a Christian. There has been a Judaeo-Christianity: in her beginnings the primitive Church was essentially established by Jews who remained wholly Jewish, except for the fact that they recognized Jesus Christ to be the Messiah announced by the prophets and the Son of God. Likewise, it seems extremely important to us today that the Jew be a Jew in the sense that, even within a universal family such as that of the Christians, there may be again a Jewish expression of Christianity, thus showing that Jewishness, if one can use this term, is part of the fullness of humanity.

There is also a second aspect on which Mr. Chouraqui has

rightly insisted: the Jew is one who praises God. This is something absolutely different from what I have said up to now. In the eyes of a Christian, a Jew is first of all a human type, and in this he is no different from other human types. But secondly, the Jew is one who praises God. The Jews, among all the peoples of the earth, are those who at a certain period of history were invested with a significance of an entirely different order. This significance did not result from their natural aptitudes, for I am convinced that the Jewish civilization in many respects was inferior to the great civilizations of that epoch.

Moreover, the Jews were greatly influenced first by Egyptian culture, then by Persian culture and finally by the Greek and Roman cultures. In this regard one can say, if one does not go beyond human characteristics, that the Jewish people seem to have a marked character, but one that is not exceptional. Nevertheless, the fact is that the Jew is someone exceptional. For us he is so not because of anything that results from his Jewish ethnicity in the broad sense of the word, but because he was the object of election in Abraham, of the covenant contracted by the true God, the only God, the one in whom we also believe. It was the Jew who was given the gift of the Law on Sinai and of the revelation made to the great prophets. All this rests then on an absolutely different order.

The bible very often adverts to this fact of a gratuitous gift. I need mention here only the admirable Chapter 16 of Ezekiel where Yahweh says to Israel that she was like an abandoned child, rejected by all, but that it was he who has chosen her and clothed her with his kindness.

Here we are in a domain that is no longer that of ethnology in the general sense of the word, but that of sacred history. From this viewpoint it seems normal to say, in answering the question that you asked a while ago, that an unbeliever cannot understand what a Jew is.

Sartre is absolutely incapable of understanding what a Jew is; since the ideas of a sacred history, a choice by God, a revelation, are wholly foreign to him, he necessarily overlooks what causes the Jewish people to be an exceptional people. This is also why atheistic Jews are incapable of saying what they are.

On the contrary, this is what Christians recognize. For Christians, the Jewish people is not a people like others, but a people that belongs to an order of reality within which Christianity is likewise situated. This order we call salvation history—the interventions of the true God in human history. The true God bound himself to Israel for a part of its history. I say for a part of its history because here we touch upon the essential problem we shall have to discuss. For us the Jewish people was a people apart during the 2,000 years that passed from Abraham to Jesus Christ.

In this perspective, it is evident that two factors can and should be distinguished. On the one hand, there is all that is ascribed to the Jewish people in its own consistence and in its right to be a people among other peoples. It is on this plane that everything proceeding from an anti-Semitism of a more or less racial character appears to us as absolutely contrary to the vision that we Christians have of things, even though—and we shall have to return to this—we do not deny that Christianity in certain cases has lent itself to a kind of anti-Semitism.

But the other problem, and I think the only true problem, that brings us face to face here is precisely that there is between the Jewish people and Christians a unique type of dialogue, different from the type that exists between Christians and other peoples. A Christian considers that the reality that began in Israel, not in the ethnic meaning of the term, but in the sense of the covenant of God with the Jewish people—that this reality, inaugurated within the Jewish people, has continued from the time of Jesus Christ, under the form of the fulfillment of the covenant, in the universalization that is the Church. This is in conformity with what was announced by the prophets. The covenant, made with Israel, remains perpetually the one that Israel was the first to receive. It has now been "enlarged to the limits of all nations." You are familiar with St. Paul's beautiful image representing the little Israelite group that recognized Christ as the wild olive tree, the initial and primitive tree on which nations were later grafted.

I come now to a point that I consider very important for our meeting today. It is clear that there has been a period of time that is of capital importance for our dialogue, one that cannot be avoided at our starting point. What happened during the years 1 to 30 of our era that made a certain group of Jews—perfectly authentic Jews, Galilean fishermen and members of priestly families—separate themselves from the rest of the Jewish people and establish that little community, consisting at first only of Jews, which later became Christianity in its various branches?

It is evident that there is here a fundamental problem, and it seems to me that it would be interesting, after this first statement of positions, for us to try today to make it clear. By means of the elements at our disposal, and in a perfectly objective manner that can clearly express what occurred (in this regard there is not a Jewish point of view and a Christian one), we may come to know just how things happened. This is essential in order to give a fundamental basis to our dialogue.

CHOURAQUI—What you have said is so rich that I do not know where to begin in order to reply and to advance our dialogue.

First of all, I believe both of us here see what is exceptional in Israel's past. Each people has a particular destiny. Israel's, on account of the importance it had in the development of universal history, was entirely special and in certain respects even extraordinary. You were speaking of the ethnic character of biblical Israel. The people of the bible were formed in a paradoxical manner in the course of the thousand years between Abraham and David. They were formed not from a starting point of ethnicity, but by the appeal of a message, a God, a covenant.

We see the people of Israel established by successive generations of men who came forth, as they do today, from the midst of neighboring civilizations. Modern Israel has revived the process of the formation of biblical Israel; men, issuing from different countries and civilizations, come to mix and integrate themselves in a land that they have chosen and decided upon.

The message of Israel, its bible, is the only vestige that we keep of Israel's past. During 1,500 years, the Jews did only one thing—they wrote not one book but a collection of books, and if the process of the establishment of Israel is paradoxical, its God is also paradoxical. St. Paul, whom you quoted, spoke of "Christian foolishness." Well, I believe we indeed share the same folly, in the sense that the God we adore, the God of Abraham, of Isaac and of Jacob, has done all that was necessary not to be the God of the philosophers or of the masses, if only because he requires, from the weak beings that we are, holiness, purity, truth and unity, that is, almost everything contrary to what instinctive and natural man habitually is. We have a paradoxical God, a paradoxical law and paradoxical aspirations by the spiritual man to surpass the carnal man. In my eyes, these paradoxes are surpassed by the fact that a small nation, a little group of men lost in the sands of the Near East, recognized themselves in this God in spite of everything, that they accepted this Law, and that they submitted their whole being and their whole life to them. For Israel, even in its infidelities, even in its betrayals, is subordinated to God and to the Law. It is bound, with its share of shadows and of light, to this Law and this God. Before all else one can affirm that Israel—and this is true not only for the Christian but objectively true in itself—is in the view of history a theophorus people, a God-bearing people, a people to whom God reveals himself and who bears this God. And now allow me to say that your vocabulary on an important point calls forth a reservation on my part, a reservation that I must emphasize for the clarity of the dialogue.

You speak of the Old Testament, and I know that your thought goes beyond this terminology inherited from a past that we must not forget but rather surpass. You know very well that Jesus did not introduce any absolute line of demarcation between the Old and the New Testaments. You know perfectly well that the majority of concepts and ideas expressed in the New Testament preexist in the Old Testament, and the ideas, later developed in the wake of the Christian event, were contained not only in the Jewish tradition of the pre-Christian century, but also, if only in germinal form, in the fabulously rich book we call the Tanah, that is, the Torah, the five books of Moses, the books of the prophets and the hagiographies.

In the new attitudes that we are irresistibly urged to take, all of us have the duty of revising our vocabulary. That Testament and that Law, which became clearly defined between the time of Moses and the epoch of the second Temple, rest on the fundamental notions you have mentioned: the notion of a personal and transcendent God, bearer of a law of love and of holiness, who offers to the people of Israel and to humanity a covenant, an alliance.

What I would wish to insist upon, because it seems to me very important, is that the covenant of the Old Testament, of the Hebrew bible, is not a closed covenant, as is too often claimed. Biblical Israel did not turn in upon itself. You say, and with good reason, that the Christian covenant is open to the whole of humanity, but if you open the bible to Chapter 9 of Genesis, you will find that the covenant proposed by God to Noah is essentially a universal covenant. The covenant is proposed to us as a pyramid. Humanity being what it is, God reveals himself to a people and charges this people with a special task to bear witness to his truth. This election made, proposed or offered to Israel does not exclude all humanity, even though there is only a part of humanity that participates consciously in this offering.

This is very important for the dialogue we are going to have on the second part of the history of Israel. We can both admire in silence the first part of the history of Israel, I because I am a Jew, you because you are a Christian. Together we recognize the transcendence of this history, the exceptional, paradoxical and unique character of this past, even with its shadows and its limitations. What divides us is what came after. But here also I would like to make another reflection.

Bossuet in his *Discourse on Universal History* states that the destiny of the Jews as the chosen people ended at the moment that Christ appeared. This is what you also do in a certain measure. You say that we were chosen until the appearance of Christ, and that then the choice passed to the Church, which became the new Israel. I think that such is your thought; at any rate it is the classic thought among Christians. Here I must say that the Jewish view is different. If I do not stress this at the very beginning, we would start with a misinterpretation, a misunderstanding.

For the Jew there is an historic continuity from Abraham even to our day. The most striking confirmation of this continuity is that our children in Jerusalem today speak the language that was spoken in Israel at the time of King David 3,000 years ago. I am sure that you do not know what language your ancestors spoke 3,000 years ago. But we Jews continue to speak today in the language of the bible.

DANIÉLOU—I am in agreement with what Mr. Chouraqui has just explained, and I find that it furnishes an excellent introduction to the deepening of our dialogue. It is perfectly true that Christianity is situated in the prolonging of all the great categories of thought enumerated by Mr. Chouraqui: the concept of the transcendence of God, the God of love, that of election, that of covenant. But here I would like to clarify a point. Mr. Chouraqui has stressed what an exceptional book the bible is, but I say it is an exceptional book precisely from the point of view of these religious affirmations. In other respects, I must say that the great masterpieces—for example, those of Greece—appear to me to have played a very important role in the history of humanity from the standpoint of civilization. The world of modern science, which is undeniably immense, has come forth from the Greek physicists. On the plane of these human efforts, there is something in Judaism that is important but not exceptional.

On the other hand, there was something wholly exceptional, namely, the conception of God and of the relations with God that existed in Israel, and at that time only in Israel. One of the things that cause Christians to consider the message of Israel as keeping a permanent character is the denunciation of idols. By this I mean that in Israel alone, at a time when the entire world was given to idolatry, there was a denunciation of every kind of idolatry as well as the affirmation that Yahweh alone is God and that all the rest is a creature of God.

CHOURAQUI—If you permit me, I am going to bring water to your mill. Let us go back to the literature of the 1st and 2nd centuries before the Christian era. Because the Jews were the only people that did not adore idols, the idolatrous nations—the Greeks and the Romans, for example—considered the Jews to be an atheistic people.

DANIÉLOU—Of course. The reason is that the Jews rejected the divinities of the State on whom the civilization was founded. Moreover, for this reason, in our own times a certain number of theologians of the State reproach the Jews, saying that they are a disintegrating element. The God of Israel is not the ideology of a State. He is transcendent to all States.

To return to what we were saying, what is therefore essential in the heritage of Israel, what Christians wholly accept and receive, is everything that results from the conception of God and the relations of humanity with God. This brings me to a problem that appears to me fundamental to our debate. What separates the Jews from the Christians is not the conception of God or the ensemble of any representations of a religious order. Even today we are living by the basic Jewish categories: *Emet* (Truth), or conformity to the designs of God; *Hesed* (Loving Kindness), which is essentially fidelity and a communication of life; *Tsedek* (Justice), in the sense that justice, as André Nehr has admirably said in his fine book on Amos, is conformity not simply to the individual right of persons, but to the totality of the design of God.

We live by these things; they still represent for us the substance of our thought, and we have denied nothing of this heritage. But it is here that I come back to the question of the historic event that took place around the first years of our era. If the distinction between Jews and Christians does not come from the conceptions, it comes essentially from the interpretation of them. Here is what I mean.

It is evident that Christianity is entirely situated within the framework of the whole revelation of God in the Old Testament. But it is situated also in the prolongation of one of the aspects of the Old Testament to which we have made no allusion up to now. Yet this aspect is of capital importance inasmuch as it is one of the traits that most separate the biblical message from the pagan religions. I am referring to the prophetic aspect. It is a fundamental trait of what we call the Old Testament—let us respect this convention—to be formed not only by the books of the Law but also by the prophetic books—Isaiah, Jeremiah, Ezekiel and the minor prophets.

Now the essence of the message of the prophets is to announce that God will intervene again in the history of the world—this is what the prophets called the day of Yahweh—and that this intervention will be the full manifestation by God of his power. He will come to judge men and to free his people.

I shall add—and here we approach more closely to our subject and touch upon the chief problem—that this hope was particularly intense in the Judaism of the two centuries before our era. This was the time of the occupation of Israel, first by the Greeks and then by the Romans, and we see the appearance of an extraordinary literature, none of which is included in the Old Testament, with the exception of the Book of Daniel. The manuscripts of Qumram have given extraordinary testimony to this immense apocalyptic literature.

It shows us that there was among the oppressed Jews an intense expectation of the intervention of God who would deliver them. The message of the Teacher of Righteousness, that great Jewish figure of the 1st century before Christ whom we have just discovered, was precisely to say that the final days had begun and that judgment was close at hand.

I stress this aspect. We can understand nothing of the Judaeo-Christian dialogue if we do not center it at this point. Therefore, there was at that moment an expectation of the eschatological event, of the action of God intervening in human history in order to save his people, to render judgment, to establish a new heaven and a new earth.

The dialogue is centered on this question of the coming of the last days, of the fulfillment of Israel's hope, for where is the point —I shall say the only point—of divergence between Jews and Christians if not here? The Jews at that time were awaiting the event foretold by the prophets. Now the whole message of Jesus when he said, "I have come not to destroy but to accomplish," and "the kingdom of God is already here," was that the event foretold by the prophets had come. This was likewise the message of the apostles who were themselves Jews and who constantly referred to the prophets—Isaiah is the most frequently quoted work in the New Testament. Unlike the Teacher of Righteousness, Jesus was not simply a great prophet, but the irruption into the world of the eschatological event, the action of God announced by the prophets.

The fundamental dialogue is situated around this interpretation given to the person of Jesus. As you know—and Jules Isaac has well recalled it to us—Jesus was much loved by a part of the Jewish people of his time. We must not think that there was a massive hostility toward him. The Jewish crowds admired him as a great religious figure; moreover, I must say, many Jews of our time admire his moral grandeur—I am thinking of men like Fleg and Isaac; I am thinking of you yourself. . . .

CHOURAQUI—Martin Buber, Rosenzweig. . . .

DANIÉLOU—They have said many beautiful things on this subject. We must never say that the Jews did not love Jesus. On the contrary, there is in present-day Judaism a current of thought that recognizes Jesus as a great figure in the history of Israel.

But the decisive moment was at the trial of Jesus, at the trial which, I think, was legal. After a certain number of witnesses had brought testimony that was not accepted, a witness appeared who said, "This man said: 'Destroy this temple and I shall rebuild it after three days.'" At that moment, the high priest tore his garments, saying, "He has blasphemed." He had indeed understood that Jesus was claiming a dignity equal to that of the Temple, that is, he was declaring himself to be the presence of God. Likewise, when Christ said that he was above the Sabbath, the Pharisees said, "He has blasphemed." This expression reoccurs almost like a *leitmotif*.

The Jews recognized perfectly—this seems to me incontestable —that Jesus was claiming an authority by which he placed himself on the same level as Yahweh himself. Now, it is clear that in the presence of this claim there are only two attitudes possible: either to say that he blasphemed—for as we said a while ago, what was strongest in Israel was the denunciation of idolatry, and the worst idolatry is for man to make himself God—or to accept that the really impossible was the truth and that Jesus had the right to claim a power equal to that of Yahweh because he was equal to Yahweh.

I remember having a discussion one day with a rabbi who said to me: "Father, there is something for which we Jews cannot help reproaching Jesus; it is that he changed the Law, for the Law was established by Yahweh, and Yahweh alone can modify what he has established." I answered: "Rabbi, you could not tell me anything that would constitute a more precious testimony, for by saying that, you recognize in effect that in modifying the law Jesus claimed an authority equal to that of Yahweh."

The problem or, more precisely, the drama that separates Jews and Christians here—a drama, however, that is on a very high plane, for it is concerned with the highest things of humanity and has nothing to do with sordid conflicts—is really this: that for a Jew either Jesus is a blasphemer, and consequently he ought to be rejected, or he is, as the Christians believe, truly the one foretold by the prophets of the Old Testament.

It is certain that Jesus placed himself absolutely in a continuous line with the prophets of the Old Testament. He explained himself only by the Old Testament; he never defined himself except in reference to the Old Testament. Jesus has never said anything but this: "I am the one announced by the prophets." Consequently, one can say that there is in Jesus nothing but the Old Testament, except for his affirmation that he was the one foretold by the prophets. This gives Christians the right to state that they are situated in the authentic prolongation of the message of the prophets of the Old Testament.

At this point I come certainly to fundamental problems, problems to which you have just led us in stating first of all that on the plane of concepts, thoughts and categories there is a full continuity. The problem is not at all that there might be a Christian mentality different from a Jewish mentality, but that the Jews have to make themselves clear in regard to Jesus, and that certain ones recognize in him the one foretold, while others do not recognize him as such. Now, there is no other question for a Christian, absolutely no other, but to know whether Jesus really is the Son of God.

CHOURAQUI—It is Jesus himself, however, who declared: "It is not he who says, Lord, Lord. . . ." You have just summed up, Father, with your habitual talent, the classic conception, the classic vision that the Church has of the Jewish phenomenon. In exaggerating a little, if you allow me, I believe I can sum up this vision of history in the following manner: Jesus appeared at a definite epoch—a particularly tragic epoch, as you said, in the history of Israel. He declared, "I am the second Person of the Blessed Trinity. . . ."

DANIÉLOU—Not exactly.

CHOURAQUI—As I said, I am exaggerating a little. The Jews reacted by accusing him of being a blasphemer; a trial ensued, at the end of which they crucified him. Nevertheless, no one is better placed than yourself to know that things did not happen in that way.

First of all, when you say *the Jews*—and you said it constantly —you betray historic truth and you recognize it. It was *some* Jews—and definitely, from a statistical viewpoint, a very small number of Jews—who were implicated in this tragedy. When you say *the Jews,* it is generally to reproach them with negative things, but the very faults that you mention were committed against other Jews: against Jesus, who was a Jew, and against the first Christians who were almost all Jews. Your terminology then is not very accurate.

Why do people persist in such bad habits? Because they have created stereotypes which project into the century of Jesus realities that developed much later. For example, beginning with the 4th and 5th centuries when the separation between the Church and the Synagogue was completed, there triumphed a Christianity which itself had a tendency to become monolithic. It then forcibly opposed Judaism which was tending to lose its extraordinary diversity after the triumph of the Pharisees, a triumph that resulted from the change in the historic situation due to the destruction of the Temple and the exile of the people. But this situation that the Doctors of the Church and those of the Synagogue then projected into the past did not yet exist in the century of Jesus. This is very evident.

In the century of Jesus there were not Jews on one side and Christians on the other. There were not even Jews in the present-day meaning of the term. There was a Hebrew phenomenon, a nation tragically divided against herself, suffering the weight of a Roman invader that she never succeeded in escaping in spite of decades of struggle and bloody fights. On the ideological plane, Judaism did not yet exist.

Let us take the example of the Pharisees and the Sadducees. The Sadducees, who were preponderant in the Sanhedrin, did not believe in eternal life or in oral tradition; they thus rejected the very essence of the faith of the Pharisees. The Pharisees were themselves very much divided. You know of the dispute at the time of Jesus between the school of Shamoi and the school of Hillel. There was not a point on which both sides were not in opposition, and not merely on secondary points but on fundamental doctrines. These groups were opposed to the Zealots who worked on the political plane. All groups together looked askance at the Essenes who lived in the desert and who were in opposition to the rest of the nation in dogma, faith and customs. Within each one of these sects there was a multitude of subgroups. This situation in Palestine had repercussions in the Diaspora.

Here we find a supplementary proof of the fact that the Jewish world was not turned back upon itself. At the time of Jesus, if one can believe Juster and Marcel Simon, the historians of the Diaspora, there were within the Empire almost 8 million Jews. They were Jews either by race or by conversion, for there were converts even within the emperor's entourage. The struggles in Jerusalem and in the land of Israel and the battle waged by the sects and movements in order to conquer the Diaspora reveal the reality of the Jewish world at this time. Its alleged monolithism is indeed part of the stereotypes, the clichés, which should be discarded in respect for historic truth.

On the contrary, the Jewish world revealed the fundamental plurality of a world in effervescence, a world aflame with ideas and dreams, doctrines and mystic fervor, a world dominated by a wild messianic hope. The latter did not cease at the time of Jesus. Even today I know some Jews who expect the coming of the Messiah tomorrow. Moreover, in the *Kaddish,* the famous prayer that the Jews say several times a day, they pray for the coming of the Messiah "in our days and immediately." I think that every belief in eschatology knows this vociferous claim for the last days, of the final accomplishment of time in a messianic realization.

I should like to insist on this point: the Judaeo-Christian conflict is not that of two opposing teams or armies, and if the dogmatic aspect of this conflict is important, it became so at the beginning of the 3rd century. At that time took place the monolithization, if I can use such a word, and the uniformization of Judaism and Christianity. Then they confronted each other in seeking the spiritual conquest of the Mediterranean world.

The conflict developed in a much more subtle way. Referring to Jewish sources, one can say that throughout this period the person of Jesus was not questioned by anybody. Jewish thought during all this time did not meet Christian thought. Later, when Jewish thought and Christian thought came into conflict, they did so on the level of the lowest polemics, the most dithyrambic apologetics and the most exaggerated criticism. They did not know one another, and they hated one another the more they did not speak to one another. Each knew or imagined only the worst of the other. The rule was to detest and ignore the other. But let us note this well: biblical thought, which condemned idolatry, coexisted for centuries with the Greek thought that you so justly praise, without these two worlds, Jewish and Greek, ever having truly met.

There was at the time of the second Temple some interpenetration, but in time this became extremely reduced. No less a person than Philo of Alexandria—you know him better than anyone—was on the margin of the Judaic as well as of the Hellenistic tradition. The facts are not as they are generally reported, and I believe that it is our duty as Jews and Christians to revise our positions today, particularly after the events that are occurring around us: for the Jews, the rebirth of Jerusalem after the great massacres of World War II, and for the Christians, the assembling of the Church and her reform in a world that has new dimensions.

Both Jews and Christians, you have said, are discovering Israel's past during the time of Christ. Young Jews, living in Jerusalem, can read firsthand the contemporary documents that have been discovered in the caves of the Dead Sea. The last memory that I took with me from Jerusalem was that of one of my little friends, a nine-year-old neighbor, who was learning from his school books to accept the period of Christ as part of his own history, of his personal heritage. By the force of circumstances a reconsideration of things has begun, and I believe we must immediately return to a real discussion of the stereotypes and clichés that are false to historic truth and hinder both recognition and dialogue.

The Judaeo-Christian confrontation is placed really on the teleological plane of historic finalities, rather than on the theological plane of the knowledge of God.

DANIÉLOU—Here again I shall stress all on which I am in full accord with Mr. Chouraqui. It is indeed very important to note that the confrontation of Judaism and Christianity under the form of two opposing blocs was a phenomenon that appeared rather late, both on the level of systems of thought and on that of separate communities. You were speaking of the 4th century. It is at that time that the Christians were established sociologically. Up to then they had been dispersed throughout the Roman Empire. It was at that moment, consequently, that there began to appear the antagonism of which we shall have to speak again, because it constitutes the profoundly tragic aspect of that history and which, I hope, was put to an end by Vatican Council II. But this brings us back to the beginnings.

It is very true that at that time the Jewish people were not at all a homogeneous unity on the doctrinal plane. There were a great number of sects, as you mentioned, and I do not have to come back to this.

CHOURAQUI—I would like to bring up a clarification here. You were speaking of the messianism of Jesus as the stumbling block. Well, here again this is not a stumbling block, or more precisely, it is not the only stumbling block. Prior to Jesus, at the time of Jesus and even after Jesus there were other Messiahs who appeared in Israel without arousing a schism as serious as the Judaeo-Christian schism. Rabbi Akiba, one of the greatest doctors of the Synagogue, believed in the messianism of Bar Kokba. No one ever said that Rabbi Akiba was mistaken. The Jews crucified neither Bar Kokba —it was the Romans who killed him—nor Rabbi Akiba—it was likewise the Romans who made a martyr of him. Not the Jews. Never were the Jews opposed to one another on a dogmatic level because they failed to recognize the Messiah in a definite person. The adventure of Sabbatai Zevi proves this sufficiently.

DANIÉLOU—To continue what I was saying. . . .

CHOURAQUI—Excuse my interruption.

DANIÉLOU—No, not at all. It is going to be of service to me in a minute. The Christians appeared in a Jewish environment; they themselves belonged in their origins to different Jewish spheres. There were certainly some Essenes among the first Christians. Others, like the fishermen of Galilee, belonged to different groups. One of the apostles was called Jude the Zealot. Cullmann has made a study of the various origins of the apostles. It is important to make clear that Christianity appeared within a Jewish environment and all its problematics were Jewish problematics.

Just the same, I feel I must slightly correct some of your statements. The feeling of separation appeared earlier than you have said. You know that the expression "the Jews" does not appear in the three synoptic gospels, where it is always a question of the Pharisees and the Sadducees. On the other hand, in St. John's gospel, which is later, but not later than the end of the 1st century, there is already question of "the Jews." This reflects a situation that had already evolved, and it shows us a world where it appears certain that, contrary to what the first apostles had believed, the Jewish people as a whole did not acknowledge Jesus.

St. John's gospel echoes the situation in which this had not happened; the Jewish people had not recognized Jesus. At this time a division appeared, and we can say that the expression "the Jews" designates the fact that the Jews as a whole had not recognized Jesus. Therefore, the Christians who were Jews, together with the pagans who had joined them, appeared to form an entity confronting the Jewish people as a whole. Without this we could not explain the difference between the synoptics, which represent the first period when no division seemed yet to exist, and the end of the century, when very clearly the die had been cast. At that period it was no longer thought that the Jews as a whole would acknowledge Jesus, which had certainly been his hope. He had announced to all the Jewish people the message of which he was the depositary, and he had certainly desired to see all the Jews recognize who he was. This was likewise the hope of the first apostles.

Therefore, there had been then a change in the situation, and a distinction appears at this time between the two kinds of Jews: the small handful of Jews who had acknowledged Jesus, and all the other Jews who had not done so. In this sense the very name "Christians" designates no one but the Jews who recognized Jesus. Therefore, it is only around the person of Jesus, and not by any means around some difference of mentality, culture or conception of God, that the separation took place.

I shall immediately add something of great importance in regard to what you said about messianism. In this first exchange of thought, what we are trying to do is to clarify a certain number of categories. It is often confusion that hinders a dialogue from being truly valuable: that is, a dialogue where words have their exact meaning. What causes the problem in regard to Jesus is not messianism as such. As you have well noted, there have been in the course of Israel's history a certain number of men who presented themselves as Messiahs. Thus the word "Messiah," signifying one anointed by Yahweh, could designate rather varied types of men. There is a continual messianism. During the Middle Ages, and even up to the 16th century, there were men who believed themselves clothed with a messianic dignity. From this point of view, Hasidism is extremely interesting.

But what I was saying a moment ago is something different. Jesus did not simply say that he was *a* Messiah like so many others, or even that he was *the* Messiah—that is, the one coming to finish the work of the Old Testament. You said that the God of Israel was a scandal, and you quoted St. Paul. But if St. Paul spoke of foolishness, it was not in regard to Yahweh; it was in regard to Christ. The complete phrase states that Jesus is "a scandal to the Jews and foolishness to the Gentiles." What was that scandal? As I said just a little while ago, it was the declaration by Jesus of his equality with Yahweh. And we must recognize that this truly was a scandal. It is quite reasonable that the Jews should have had so much difficulty in acknowledging Jesus. From this point of view, there have been statements concerning the guilt of the Jews that the Council has now rectified, and with good reason.

The problem must be rigorously posed. Recall the exalted idea that the Jews had of the transcendence of Yahweh. It is evident that if a man, whose mother and cousins were known, by declaring himself the Master of the Law and the Master of the Sabbath, let it be understood that he had the right to forgive sins and that he had a dignity equal to that of Yahweh, this was for the Jews absolute scandal. The gospels prove in an absolute manner that Christ made these assertions.

At that moment there was a break, not simply on the plane of the messianism of a prophet, but on the plane of what Jesus allowed to be glimpsed and of what Christians believe: namely, not only that he was a very great Messiah who was separating himself from Judaism in order to found a new branch that would in the end reattach itself to Israel, but also that he was really the eschatological event foretold by the prophets—that is, the coming of Yahweh himself, under a form unexpected but nevertheless real.

The whole question is here, and for a Jew this remains a scandal. But the problem here is one of the faith in the risen Christ that is common to all men and not that of the responsibility for the crucifixion of Jesus.

CHOURAQUI—It has been implied. . . .

DANIÉLOU—On that I am fully in accord with you. There is an erroneous conception of Israel's collective responsibility in regard to the death of Jesus, and it has been rightly denounced by the Council. But it remains true that there is a scandal for Israel in the declarations of Jesus, and this continues even today. Otherwise there would be no reason for our separation. This permits us to lay bare the real, important and mysterious center of the debate, and thereby to free it from all the sordid questions on which we shall have to express ourselves later in order to show how much misunderstanding and injustice there has been in this tragic story. We cannot minimize, however, that there is a real problem between us. My sole preoccupation is to say here what is the real problem, and then we shall be able to say precisely what the false problems are that we can work to suppress.

CHOURAQUI—I do not mean to suppress any real problem. Nevertheless, like you, I know the story. The Judaeo-Christian dialogue starts out in spite of the affirmation of the divinity of Jesus, which is a scandal in the eyes of a Jew, and in spite of the refusal of the Jew to acknowledge the person of Jesus, which is not less scandalous in the eyes of the Christian. As a result of this double scandal, each one bristles, and all too often after the Christian has stated all his reasons for his belief in the divinity of Christ and the Jew has answered with all his arguments to prove the non-divinity of Christ, the dialogue becomes congealed.

This was the case in a particular Judaeo-Christian controversy at the court of the Count of Toulouse in the Middle Ages. The Count became angry and, unsheathing his sword, he declared: "Jew, you will have no answer to this argument." He then cut off the Jew's head. It should be evident that I do not wish to come to that!

DANIÉLOU—I hope not!

CHOURAQUI—I do not wish to come to that, not for the safety of my own neck, but for the truth that should unite us. If we truly wish to carry on a dialogue, we must penetrate into the thought of one another. To penetrate into the thought of Christians who have proclaimed since the coming of Christ into the world that Jesus is God is an effort that can be made by any mind, even a Jewish one. Moreover, all that we know now of Jewish thought at the time of Christ allows us to see that this idea of the miraculous birth of the man of God, the divine birth of the man of God, is not an exclusively Christian idea. You are a specialist in Philo of Alexandria, and you know that Philo in *De Fideo* declares that the high priest of Jerusalem is the son of God and *Sophia* (Wisdom). Philo was sent by the Jews of Alexandria to plead the Jewish cause in Rome. They did not crucify him because he had said this, and they did not crucify the high priest. . . .

DANIÉLOU—Exactly. That proves how widespread all ideas are, and that the real problem is a problem of fact. The Jews admitted in fact that God could intervene in the world, and they still believe it today. . . .

CHOURAQUI—Likewise the birth of the patriarchs and the illustrious men of the bible is always announced by the words *Eloim pakad*—God visited Sarah, God visited Rebecca, God visited Rachel. This visitation of God always announced the birth of a hero.

For a long time one believed that monastic life was the invention of the Christians. Now the discovery of the Dead Sea scrolls gives us the link that was formerly lacking. We know that the monastic life was also accepted and recommended by certain Jews. Here, too, there is a closer relationship between Jews and Christians than used to be admitted.

It is impossible to carry on a dialogue if you say to me, "You are a scandal for me," and if I reply, "You are a scandal for me." On these positions nothing remains but to draw the sword. Now we can no longer do even that. We have at most only pens in our hands. Our intentions also have changed; they have become different in a wonderfully changed universe.

In order that you may be able to penetrate into the thought of the Jew, I should like to say this to you. You are trying to reduce the Judaeo-Christian dialogue to a dialogue of ideas, and this, in my opinion, is very un-Christian. Christians are not idealists or nominalists; men who believe in the God of Abraham, Isaac and Jacob do not believe solely in "ideas." Their importance must not veil the global reality of man incarnate; very often this global reality of man goes beyond what he himself knows of it. There is a mystery of the Jew as there is a mystery of man; our existence is always placed beyond our thoughts.

I should like to say this about the existence of the Jew. Your thought seems to fail to recognize the permanence of the Jew as he is. If there is a paradox of biblical Israel (and this biblical Israel, at least, you recognize, acclaim and extol), there is an exilic Israel with a mystery as great, and this one you do not know. Perhaps it is the fault of us Jews that you do not know it. I insist on this because even in the Christian problematic exilic Israel has a meaning at least as great—and in Christian historicism and existence at least as necessary—as the biblical Israel.

I must explain myself. First of all, it seems to me that everything proves that exilic Israel should have disappeared after the great massacres of the Jews by the Romans. Tacitus, generally a cautious historian, places the number of Jewish victims in the war against the Romans at 600,000 men—600,000 men *crucified*. Jesus was crucified, but in addition to him, according to Tacitus, there were 600,000 Jews who were hung on crosses by the Romans during the combat that went on during the years 66 to 134. This forest of crosses you do not keep in mind, but we Jews have not forgotten it. A Russian proverb says: "A hundred blows of the rod on the back of a neighbor is a real pleasure." One has much more difficulty in forgetting the blows received on one's back, even if it did happen 2,000 years ago. The 600,000 Jews crucified by the Romans remain unforgettable for us; they mark the origin of the great deportation of the Jews, just as the 6,000,000 victims of Hitler mark the return of Israel to the Holy Land.

Now in the economy of the Roman world, these Jews, deprived of a country, deprived of a common language, deprived of all help and quickly tracked down by everyone, should have disappeared. One should now remember the Jews of the biblical epoch in the same manner as one remembers the Palmyrians of the glorious era of Palmyra: that is, as a reality that has disappeared. Now the Jewish phenomenon has continued and has developed in an extremely paradoxical way, the more paradoxical as the Jews who survived the great massacres and the Roman deportation withdrew within themselves in an unsocial way. They survived contrary to all laws of history.

One could hold forth for hours on the paradox represented by the survival of the Jews of the Diaspora. Beginning with the second millennium of the Christian era, the existence of the Jews was rendered almost impossible by the conditions imposed upon them in Europe as well as in the Moslem countries. Let us remark here that there were Jews only within the frontiers formed by monotheism in the geography of the world—in the Christian empire on one side, and in the Moslem empire on the other. Among the Moslems as well as among the Christians—and more often among the Christians than among the Moslems—the Jew lived in a marginal, often tragic situation. He was harried, tracked down, persecuted, discriminated against and often killed.

On the other hand, the Moslems promised him a place in paradise if he would be converted. Among the Christians, too, conversion was sometimes matched with promises much more concrete. In certain Nordic countries, a barony or a county was offered to Jews who consented to be converted. The paradox is that, faced with a choice between the fire of hell, the fire of an earthly hell, the fire of the stake, or prosperity in this life and in the beyond, the Jew, despite everything, clung to his Judaism that promised him only abjection. An abjection that we have known.

I am a man who has seen 6,000,000 victims burned around him, killed simply because they were Jews. This is not in ancient history. I have quoted Tacitus with the 600,000 victims of the Romans, but Hitler has multiplied this number by ten. You know enough of these Jews who were burned, trod upon, massacred, of those Jewish children—1,800,000 children under fourteen—who were assassinated because they were Jews. This happened in a land that had been Christianized for 2,000 years.

Why such relentlessness? In 1942, when I was in the underground and pursued by the Germans, a doctor from Clermont-Ferrand asked me one day: "Why the devil do you persist in being Jews?" Oh yes, why the devil? Why the devil have we persisted for 2,000 years to defy all the laws of history, to bear the bitterness, the hatred, at times the murderous folly, of almost all nations simply to remain Jews? Is that worth the trouble? Were we so totally insane that we accepted this condition and took up the challenge? And when the doctor of Clermont-Ferrand, at the time when the Gestapo was at my heels because I was a Jew, asked me, "Why the devil do you persist?", I asked myself this question, "Is it worth all the trouble?" So much blood, so much suffering, the weight of which we bear! If the Inquisition is responsible for the blood it shed, its victim remains irreducibly linked to it by the situation that both in a certain way agreed to create. Juda Halévy insisted on the fact that the Jews have freely chosen to submit to the Calvary of exile. The Jews—and I am one—who lived during the war at the entrance of crematory furnaces, in a certain way not only submitted but accepted the madness of the Hitlerian murderers, and I mean to be understood. Is it worth so much pain, so much blood, so many tears, so many iniquities aroused by our obstinacy?

Can this drama be reduced to a theological quarrel, debating
whether Jesus was in a small measure, not at all, or entirely the
Messiah? Is there a common measure between this idea, this theological debate in regard to a mystery, on one side, and, on the
other side, so much blood connected with the destiny of a part of
humanity? I should not wish to see the "why" of all this in the
blindness of the Jew opposing the Christian, or of the Church
opposing the Synagogue. In your cathedrals, Father, there are
often two statues: one of the triumphant Church and one of the
Synagogue. Very often, as in the cathedral of Strasbourg, the
sculptors had the kindness to represent the Synagogue with traits
much more elegant than those of the Church. But have you noticed
the veil on the face of the Synagogue that is intended to signify its
blindness? That veil also hides the Synagogue's face that one sur-
mises is subtle and beautiful. Has the Church uncovered this face?
If there is any blindness, I believe that it is reciprocal—blindness
of the Jews in regard to the Christian reality, and blindness of the
Church in regard to the Judaic reality.

I should like to say what in my eyes is the essential significance
of this Judaic reality by quoting Juda Halévy, an author of the
Middle Ages and one of the great Jewish poets of the Exile, as
great as one can be in the tradition of the bible. Halévy is the
author of an admirable book, written in Arabic, and now being
translated into French. Often the great Jewish theologians of the
Middle Ages expressed themselves in the vernacular of the country
in which they were; at that time in Spain it was Arabic. This book
is entitled *Apology for the Despised Religion,* and you undoubtedly know it under the name of *Kuzari.* It has for its theme an
historic fact. One day a king named Kasar, wishing to be instructed
in the truths of religion and philosophy, summoned an imam, a
priest, a philosopher and a rabbi. The imam, the philosopher and
the priest instructed the king in the realities of their faith. Then
came the turn of the Jew. He began his apology by saying: "Formerly Israel had a Temple and priests that constituted the heart
and the head of Israel." You are sufficiently informed about biblical
truths to know that in reality the whole structure and the spiritual
economy of Israel rested then on the Temple and on the priests.

The king Kasar replied at once: "Today you have neither Temple nor priests. You are therefore a people without a head and without a heart." The Jewish theologian's answer was to say to King Kasar: "You have said it. We are not only a people without a head and a heart, but we are a bundle of dried-up bones. And such is our dignity. The Christian and the Mohammedan have made an apology of the despised condition, the abjection, of what you call the cross. But we, the Jews, bear this cross; we incarnate this humiliated state." In this vein of thought, we must recognize that at the side of the 600,000 crucified by the Romans, in the blood and mud of centuries, there has been an immense crowd of Jews crucified in order to bear witness to a certain honor in man. I should like you to become aware of this! When a man, a Jew, is assassinated, does not his blood spurt up on your hands as on mine?

DANIÉLOU—I should like to say, first of all, to Mr. Chouraqui what a deep echo the words he has just said awaken in me and in every Christian. This drama of Israel through all the years of exile and the various responsibilities that have existed in this drama—including those of Christians that we fully acknowledge—are the very occasion of our dialogue. It is evident today that something new is stirring. This something, on the morrow of the atrocities of the Hitlerian regime, is the consciousness that such things should not exist. The awakening of the Christian conscience to the problem of Israel ought to be an established fact. These are questions that we shall have to speak of again. Nevertheless I want to insert a twofold remark here.

Mr. Chouraqui began by saying: "We remain with problems of ideas, and in reality the important problem is the problem of the fact of the Jew." I think—and this is joined to the question that we asked just now—that there is indeed a human problem, a problem of the Jew inasmuch as it is a human problem, and this we absolutely have to face, for it is a grave problem.

But I think it would be inadmissible on the part of a Jew to say that what concerns fundamental religious declarations is something that should not be considered as having an equally sovereign importance. The Judaeo-Christian dialogue is not a dialogue that takes place only on the plane of the problems of civilization, however serious these are. In my opinion, we minimize the importance of this dialogue if we do not think of it as being also on the plane of the fundamental destiny of humanity, that is, of what is important for all of us.

We think that the essential problem—and this a Jew believes as fully as a Christian or a Moslem—is not simply to establish a civilization among men that would be as fraternal as possible; it is the problem of anti-Semitism, and on this point I am in full accord. However, the problem is also to know what is finally the destiny of man. That is why on my side I will absolutely refuse to call this latter problem one of ideas and to minimize its importance.

I believe that what Jews and Christians, working together, have to recall to the world, to the world that more and more is enclosing itself in a universe cut off from God, is that the relation to a living God is part of the very fullness of life, and that men have as much need of God, of the true God, as they have need of bread and lodging. To be false to this seems to me one of the most intolerable things for a Jew as well as for a Christian. It would be to minimize the importance of the religious dimension of man in order to draw attention only to questions, however fundamental they may be, that concern the organization of the earthly city. I do not in any respect think that the order of the questions we have approached a while ago can be minimized. This order remains fundamental from the human point of view. It is this that the Old Testament proclaims from the beginning to end.

This said, we have now abruptly crossed over one stage. We had decided today that we should speak of the problem of origins, and Mr. Chouraqui has thrown us right into the problem of the exile that I feel should be discussed at another time. Are we tackling today this enormous question of anti-Semitism? Really, it is an enormous question! Would it not be better to finish our conversation about the first part and admit that the problem raised by Mr. Chouraqui is a fundamental problem to which we shall devote an entire talk?

CHOURAQUI—I believe that the two problems to which you refer are closely linked. Exilic Israel is bound to the problem of the origins of the Judaeo-Christian conflict. To my mind, it is first necessary to define the real choice set before the Jews of the 1st, 2nd and 3rd centuries, at the time that the boundaries between the Church and the Synagogue were still undetermined. During that epoch, dogmatic positions were not wholly defined, either within the Church or within the Synagogue. The Church was struggling between different tendencies—that of Peter, that of Paul, those of the various heresies. The Jews were torn between the opposing tendencies of the Sadducees and the Pharisees, the latter finally winning out but with difficulty and only after centuries of struggle. The real choice placed before the Jews of those three centuries was not whether to declare Jesus as God, but rather whether it was worth the trouble to assure the continuity of the Jew.

To assure the continuity of the Jew was for the Israelite a problem vital to his heart. For each Jew, then, all that mattered was whether or not to assume the heritage of Israel. Inversely, Jesus was totally absent from the Jewish problem of that time. Here and there are notes in the Talmud, allusions so well veiled that we are not sure whether they refer to Jesus or to someone else. On the other hand, the central problem, that of assuring the survival of Israel, is found in all the sources. The Roman victory was considered by the Jews as the inevitable chastisement of their iniquity. All the sources recognize the justice of God. The Jews deserved what they got, the defeat they experienced at the hands of the Romans. They merited it because they had been unfaithful to their God and divided among themselves. No one questioned the judgment of God when he crushed the nation. Theirs was an heroic defeat in the face of Rome, since it stopped the Roman expansion toward Asia. Between the years 66 and 134, the Romans experienced the most abject failure in their military history, and this was inflicted on them by the Jews against whom they had sent their best armies and their best generals—Pompey, Titus and their legions. The Jews were finally crushed, but they dominated their conquerors obliquely through the Christian victory. The Romans broke their idols to adore the God of Abraham, Isaac and Jacob.

The problem for the Jew was to know whether he should accept his defeat and disappear or persist in being a Jew. To continue to be a Jew implied, therefore, a theological choice that committed God himself. The Jew of that epoch believed that he had well deserved his national defeat. However, he refused to believe that God would be false to his Word and his Promise. I shall cite the case of Rabbi Akiba. Before the smoking ruins of the Temple, and surrounded by his dismayed disciples, he sang and danced a few steps. His pupils looked at one another in consternation, saying: "Has Rabbi Akiba, the great doctor of the Synagogue, gone mad because too much misfortune has overwhelmed him?" The master guessed their thoughts and said to them: "Sons, I dance a few steps not because I have lost my reason, but because it is written in the prophets that the Temple would be destroyed. I rejoice to see the Temple destroyed, because this gives authenticity to the scriptures which also foresaw that the Temple would be rebuilt and that redemption would come for all Israel and for all humanity." His joy sprang from this certitude. But in order that the Word should be accomplished, one condition was necessary—Israel must survive.

Think again of the structures of the ancient world. Israel could survive only by separating itself from the nations. Therefore, after the exile, Israel retired within itself, separating itself from the whole world. The Jew said "no" to the Christian; he said "no" to the Roman world; he said "no" to Greek philosophy; later he said "no" to Islam, although this was closer to him and often more fraternal. He said "no" to all; he refused to accept the world about him, not through a madness of negation or a mania for refusals, but in order to preserve his sole chance of survival.

If he said "yes" to any other thing, he immediately ceased to be a Jew. The Jews who said "yes" to Greek philosophy became Greeks; the Jews who said "yes" to the Church became Christians; those who said "yes" to Islam—and very many did—ceased to be Jews. The true choice, it seems to me, was not in regard to the person of Christ, but rather in the acceptance of another Calvary, that of exile, which at least preserved the existence of Israel and safeguarded the chances of a redemption that would fulfill the Promise. Nietzsche said he believed witnesses who signed with their blood. Here blood, at least, was not lacking, if any was needed to make the testimony authentic.

If there is to be a dialogue between Jews and Christians, each group must first penetrate the thought of the other. You are always centering your arguments on the person of Christ, thereby stressing the significance of the Jews' refusal, without perceiving perhaps the deepest and truest reasons for that refusal. These reasons must be seen in a truly unique historic situation and perhaps also in a certain exaggerated claim of the absolute. I have quoted Jesus saying: "Not everyone who says to me, 'Lord, Lord,' shall enter the kingdom of heaven, but he who does the will of my Father in heaven shall enter the kingdom of heaven" (Mt. 7, 21).

Painters, authorized by the Church, do not hesitate to represent Christians and even princes of the Church burning in the fires of hell. I suppose that in the Christian paradise there must be some good pagans, and I hope some Jews. Jesus said also that there are several mansions in his Father's house. We must therefore try to look beyond our frontiers and our steeples to the great destiny of humanity. I am not for a syncretism that results from confusion; I am not for smoothing out difficulties by burying them in the sands of a misunderstanding; but I am for a real dialogue such as has become inevitable today. A true dialogue does not come into being through scandal, opposition or violence. It supposes a fundamental step—that of penetrating into the thought of the other to discover its real basis. A dialogue requires respect on the part of each speaker and an inner silence that is attentive to find in the other a deeper thought that would be in accord with a pattern of the history of mankind; for creation reveals a will transcending our world of ideas which at times veils the face of God if love is absent.

I should like to add one further thought. Reread the gospels, the Torah of Moses and the predictions of the prophets and the apostles. Nowhere therein are we asked to be good Christians or good Jews, but all those sources require that we be just, upright, pure, good and charitable. Now and then we are asked to be true witnesses to a transcendent presence of love and unity, bearing this love and this unity to the world. If we have been seriously divided by the pattern of history, a day will come—may it come tomorrow —when we shall have to unite in order to assure the attainment of humanity's final goals, to secure the accomplishment of the salvation that the world is awaiting and that together we do not cease to hope for.

DANIÉLOU—On that we are again in very profound agreement, and therefore I feel we should close out this sector of our discussion, saying that we have many tasks in common, and that indisputably a Christian recognizes in a number of Jews a great passion for justice and for peace among men, as well as an authentic religious passion. But I think that in bringing us back to the question of what occurred at the beginning, Mr. Chouraqui has perhaps touched upon the essential point by recalling that the Jewish problem—I believe I have understood his thought—was fundamentally the problem of the permanence of the Jew. Moreover, this is not extraneous to the problem of Jesus. The drama—for truly this constitutes a drama—was the question of knowing whether the fact of Jesus constituted a threat to the permanence of Israel. Here we touch upon an extremely difficult problem which obliges us to go back to the distinctions you yourself made a while ago that I subsequently took up.

To me it is evident that there is an aspect of Israel's permanence that Christianity in no way puts into question. It is a fact, as we said in the beginning, that Israel represents a certain ethnic element, a certain land in the widest sense of the word. This ethnic element and this land are not in any way contested by Christians. I shall say, on the contrary, that one of the most essential views of contemporary Christianity is to stress the fact that no ethnic element, no culture, no tradition is threatened by Christianity, but that, on the contrary, all find their fulfillment in it. It is in this sense that we consider, for example, that a Hindu who has been converted does not renounce in any way the religious tradition of his race, but rather fulfills it.

But what makes the problem dramatic for Israel is that Israel is not simply a race like others, but it rather represents an encounter with the living God, an encounter that is expressed through all the institutions that this living God gave to Israel. Here we approach a problem that we have not touched upon until now—that of the Jewish observances. This problem is of capital importance. You yourself mentioned that you were circumcised. We could also make allusions to the Sabbath and to all practices which, it has been said, make Judaism in many regards more an orthopraxy than an orthodoxy. It is constituted not so much by dogmas as by an assemblage of holy observances, and it is in this that the Jews are different from other peoples.

You said that the Jews had shut themselves off from all the great currents of their time. There is in the Jewish people a certain resistance to assimilation that does not exist either among the pagans, who are assimilated very easily, or among the Christians, who assimilate very easily. What is peculiar to the Jews—I am returning now to our original idea—is the existence in the same human group of a special ethnic character, on the one hand, and, on the other, a testimony given to the living God of all mankind. This causes Judaism, because it is on a higher religious plane, to present a resistance to assimilation that paganism does not present at all.

It is evident that the group of Jews who believed in Jesus were confronted with a whole series of cases of conscience when faced with the essential point you have stressed—namely, the persistence of Israel. To me this is where the drama in great part takes place. One of the cases of conscience was identification with the political drama of Israel at the time of the uprising against the Romans and at the time of the Jewish war. It is certain that at those times the Judaeo-Christians appeared to the Jews to be refusing to identify themselves with the temporal destiny of Israel. It was uncontestably one of the things that deepened the gap between them. The generally accepted fact of the departure of the Christians for Pella separated them from their brother Jews who remained in Jerusalem. They left precisely because they were conscious that they were bearers of something that was no longer simply the continuance of Judaism, but rather something which went beyond Judaism and which must be carried to the world; therefore, they felt that they did not have the right to compromise this message in identifying themselves with the temporal Israel.

However, there is a much more serious problem. I am referring to the attitude of Jesus in his earthly life in regard to religious practices. Jesus declared the coming of a spiritual Law consisting of more than observances. Circumcision and purifications were holy institutions established by Yahweh, but they did not have a definitive character. Jesus himself said to the Samaritan that from that time on God wished servants "in spirit and in truth." Moreover, this is one of the things that caused a certain type of Judaism in spirit and in truth to be attracted to the person of Jesus. On the part of the Jews who became Christians, it entailed unfaithfulness to at least one aspect of Israel's continuity that you defined just now.

But I maintain that even if all Israel had been converted to Jesus Christ, the essential of the continuity of Israel would not have been threatened. Israel has its place in the universal Church of Jesus Christ, and I hope that one day it will find it. I do not think that this menaces Israel in what constitutes the essentials of its continuity. However, it was a difficult problem, for it implied the acceptance of the fact that certain aspects of Judaism had been transcended—in particular, that of religious observances. The question has been asked whether a modern Judaeo-Christianity could keep the Sabbath, circumcision and the purifications. This seems difficult to me. The change from the Sabbath to Sunday, a question already discussed by the Fathers of the Church, would in fact impose a choice between the two. Thus one can easily see that conversion to Christianity could have appeared to the Jews a repudiation of Judaism; it presented a problem of conscience, the importance of which I do not at all minimize.

CHOURAQUI—We shall advance the more in our dialogue the better we avoid projecting into the past the realities of today. When you say that the Jew is well adapted for conversion to Christianity, you are speaking as a man of 1966 who forgets the arsenal of war forged by the Church to efface the Jew. The crime of Judaism appeared in the 4th century. It was codified in the laws of Justinian, which inspired in all of Christendom the draconian measures destined to cause the Jew as such to disappear. From that time dates what Jules Isaac has called the teaching of contempt. I believe that if one wishes to carry on a dialogue, one must discover the universe not only as it appears from his point of view, but also as it appears to his neighbor. Now the crime of Judaism was punished for centuries in Christendom in an often pitiless way. We suffered so much from the teaching of contempt, with its arsenal of discriminatory laws and its often murderous practices, that it would be improper for us to dwell on it. Christianity should become clearly conscious of this fact instead of masking its dreadful shadows. An unreserved *mea culpa,* an expression of sympathy and contrition coming from the depths of one's heart, would do more to draw souls together than all the debates in the world.

Circumstances and men have permitted the tragedies of history. This does not prevent the Judaeo-Christian conflict from revealing a real aberration of conscience. Rather than speak here of all its horror, I merely ask you to recall what some great Christians have said on this point—Jacques Maritain,[1] for example, and Popes Pius XI and John XXIII.

You have projected into the past another present-day reality. Many Jews are in agreement with you on this point—I mean the place of the Law in the economy of faith. Let us go back to the epoch of Jesus. The Jewish world was not yet a nomocracy, but a theocracy. God reigned; he was present in the Temple; his priests were his intermediaries with the people. The Law in this economy had a secondary importance. What was primary was the living God present in the Temple, the priests and the sacrifices that purified for faults committed against the Law. When the Temple disappeared, the spiritual structure of the Jewish world was completely overthrown. I should like you, first of all, and every other Christian to be aware of this revolution which transformed the very essence of Israel's spiritual life. With the Temple destroyed, Israel knew the pangs of a supreme tragedy: that of the exile of God himself.

[1] Cf. Jacques Maritain, *The Mystery of Israel.*

To suggest the extent of the upheaval wrought by the destruction of the Temple, permit me to give an analogy. Israel was
enclosed in a situation which would be similar to that of Christianity if it were deprived of sacrifice and sacraments, if all the
priests would find it impossible to say Mass and administer the
sacraments and all the bishops would be unable to ordain new
priests. With the Temple destroyed, Israel in exile was deprived of
all sacramental life; now this, since the time of Moses, was the
very essence of Judaic life. The Temple was the head and the
priests were the heart of the Jewish people. Since there was only
one Temple and one altar in Israel, when the Temple was destroyed sacramental life disappeared. Ordination and the traditional continuities ceased in Israel.

The national exile of Israel, driven from its land, is only the
image and the earthly transcription of a much more absolute exile
—that of God. God is henceforth the great Absent One for whom
the Jews are seeking. And here is an indication of what I mean.
You call God "Yahweh." Now you know very well that this name
of Yahweh is an unverifiable hypothesis of modern scholars. It is
probable, or at any rate possible, that the God of the Hebrews
bore another name. Thus we, who are a people with a long memory, have handed down the texts from century to century with
minute details. We know how many words Moses has written in
his Torah and how many sentences there are in each of the prophets. We have handed down all of the divine Word of Sinai even to
our own day with a fidelity that is in some way mechanical, a
fidelity that is emphasized by the manuscripts of the Dead Sea.
These have made us take a leap of a thousand years in the history
of texts and have proved to us the value of the Hebrew memory.
Yet we have a blank in this prodigious memory; we have forgotten
only one thing, but that thing is of great importance. We have
forgotten the name of our God. We have forgotten it because his
name had become unpronounceable since the destruction of the
Temple which plunged us into a metaphysical exile.

In this exile it was no longer faith that saved, but the Law
alone that permitted the sociological existence of those who survived exile. Several centuries before Jesus, the prophet Habacuc

had written: "The just man will live by his faith" (Hab. 2, 4). This sentence was considered by the rabbis of Israel to sum up the essence of faith. *Tsaddik be-emunato ehye:* "The just man in his faith will live." Faith in the structures of the exilic world must henceforth be articulated with the requirements of the Law.

The exile founded the exilic nomocracy. When you speak of the place of the Law in the economy of faith, you must distinguish, in regard to Judaism, the pre-exilic period and the post-exilic period. As we had nothing that survived the shipwreck of exile, the carapace we secreted in order to maintain ourselves in being was the Law. This became faith, an act of faith, since it established the continuity of Israel and created the organ that permitted the prodigious survival of the people of the bible.

But as soon as the rabbi spoke to souls (consult Bahya Ibn Paquda, an author you must know), nomocracy did not have that absolute place imputed to it, but which it does not have in any spiritual writer. The Law is situated on a sociological plane; it is the shell that permits the germ to be preserved, without thereby supplanting faith whose primacy remains complete. The Judaism of the 19th century, anxious to define itself by opposition to Christianity, may have thought the contrary; it is responsible for the doctrinal confusion that leads astray both Jews and Christians. Contemporary scholarship, especially in Israel, is reexamining these schematizations that date from that epoch, particularly the one that makes the Law the sole pivot of the spiritual life. This is true only on the sociological plane. The spiritual options are quite different and are, as Bahya has so well said, in the realm of unity and love.

There are two more details I should like to add. I believe that the divorce between the Church and the Synagogue was much more the result of historic causes than of dogmatic ones. The divorce was declared when, after Constantine's conversion, the Church identified herself with the Roman Empire, against which Israel had been at war for centuries. Rome was the enemy. Suddenly here was the head of that Roman Empire adopting the faith of one of the communities of Israel. Before Constantine's conversion, the Christian Church could appear as one of the numerous sects of the house of Israel. After his conversion, things became worse and more clear-cut. The Jews of that era had fought against the Roman Empire because the Romans were imperialists, the conquerors of their country, pagans who occupied their land with harshness and bullied them. The Jews could not take any other attitude but to be against the Roman Empire. The "collaborators," who were few, were despised. Patriotism and faith were in accord in fighting Rome. The identification of Rome with the Church, after the conversion of Constantine, undoubtedly strengthened the divorce of the Church and Synagogue. Here is something that is very deep, and I believe it is one of the knots of our problem.

Finally, I wish to add this. I have already spoken of the human value of the Judaic option, that foolish and paradoxical option which maintained the permanence of the Jews in spite of everything and everyone, even in spite of us Jews. Do you think that it is a simple and easy thing to be a Jew in this century that has seen the rise and growth of Hitler? Do you think that the Jews have lightheartedly climbed the Calvary that this century has been for them?

I believe that the permanence of the Jew is important not only for the Jews, but for all men, and this remark perhaps will lead us to the following dialogue on anti-Semitism. I may speak as a Jew, but I feel myself the involuntary author of a fact, the Judaic permanence, that keeps the fullness of its meaning for all men, or so it seems to me. If I had to sum up why, in spite of its paradox and its cost of blood, this permanence seems so important to me, I should say it is primarily because of its fidelity to the Word of God. The Jew who is the furthest away from the Word of God, by the simple fact that he exists as a Jew, remains faithful, although sometimes involuntarily and unconsciously, to the covenant of Abraham and to its permanence.

This fidelity, which I grant was often blind, has permitted Jewish history to inscribe its deed in the history of the world. Furthermore, in the history of the last millennia—more exactly, between the years 134 and 1917—the Jews constituted the only human group, *the only one,* that passed through all those years with their hands empty, with no weapons for attack and no weapons for their defense. In the 2nd century, in the year 134, after the combats of Bethar in Israel and the revolt in Libya a little later—it was the last gasp of the Jewish revolt against Rome—the Jews were definitely crushed and disarmed by the Romans.

For twenty centuries the Jews constituted a human group deprived of all means of defense. The weapons were snatched from their hands. They were not to take them up again until 1917 in Palestine, and until 1947 in Europe, at the time of the revolt in the ghetto of Warsaw. We have passed through twenty centuries of history with our hands empty, unarmed, while maintaining the most resistant of spiritual presences. Confronted with all the empires, all the nations, all the Churches, all with weapons, organized armies and means of pressure, of which we felt the weight, a small group of unarmed men were able to survive every persecution and triumph over every temptation and obstacle only by the sole virtue of their spirit. Is there not here an extraordinary testimony for our century of violence?

DANIÉLOU—At the beginning you emphasized the fact that the conflicts which developed after Constantine had their origin in Israel's resistance to the Roman Empire. You reproached me with sometimes projecting into the past the views of a modern Christian. It seems to me that in the discussion you are always interpreting the original situation in function of the situation that developed after Constantine. This falsifies the data of the problem. With Constantine we enter into a new period properly called that of Christianity, but before that time the problem was different.

First of all, we must not forget that at that time the Jews in a general way enjoyed a privileged position compared to the Christians. I am an historian of that period, and consequently I know something about it. It is historically certain that the Jewish religion was a religion recognized in the Roman Empire and that the Jews were not especially persecuted. You yourself recalled that at that period, when there were 10,000,000 Jews, almost 8,000,000 of them were living in Egypt, Mesopotamia, Asia Minor, Rome, Greece, Spain and North Africa, where they had been long before the Arabs. These Jews were not disturbed at all.

In fact, the very remarkable works of Goodenough and Marcel Simon show particularly that the view you have developed just now of an Israel resisting all exterior influences after the fall of Jerusalem is not historically exact. We have rediscovered, for example, the influence of profane art on Jewish art at the synagogue of Doura-Europa, and the works of Goodenough show how inexact is the idea of the Jews' proscription of images. They were deeply penetrated by the culture of the time.

You spoke of Philo, who was much influenced by the culture of Greece and particularly by its philosophy. There was in this epoch a harmony between Judaism and the Roman Empire. The Jews did not suffer at this time, but the Christians, on the contrary, up to the time of Constantine, experienced a situation much more precarious. They were not protected by a legal statute because their religion was not a national religion that could be recognized for a particular human group.

I stress this point, which seems to me very important, in order to avoid projecting anti-Semitism into the beginnings. This arose later in the course of centuries, but it was not at all the original situation. In the beginning, the Christians were not powerful. They were persecuted; they had their crucified and their martyrs. Their condition was more difficult than that of the Jews.

Beginning with Constantine the situation was reversed, and the Christians became the persecutors of the Jews. But you will not find a single Christian persecutor of the Jews until the time of Theodosius. How could the Christians have persecuted anyone, since they were deprived of the means of coercion? They constituted small communities that were often tracked down. Moreover, since they formed unyielding groups, they often bore the fury of certain local populations. This period should not be interpreted as though the same conditions existed then as they did in the later situation.

You have said interesting things about the way I have perhaps magnified the importance of religious observances in Judaism.

Here again, although you are more competent than I in this regard, I do not wholly agree with you. It is certain, and the first Christian texts prove it (I am thinking of some episodes in the history of St. Paul), that the problems of the Sabbath and of circumcision appeared to be a crucial problem at that time. The idea that one could belong to a Christian community without the Jewish observances was something that appeared unthinkable to both Jews and Christians.

CHOURAQUI—In the Hellenistic period there were many Jews who were not circumcised. The tenor of the Sabbatical observance for a Pharisee was quite different from what it was for a Sadducee, even at the time of Christ. The hardening of the notion of the Law that one can notice in the Hebrew tradition occurred not only later than the destruction of the Temple but even later than the time this event was admitted as definitive by the Jews, for during several decades they had hoped that the Temple would be rebuilt without delay. It is probable that sacrificial worship was continued for a certain time after the year 70.

DANIÉLOU—Yes. Nevertheless I wonder whether you are now magnifying the importance that the cult of the Temple had in relation to the Law. I am thinking, for example, of a community such as the Essenes of whom we were speaking just a while ago. They did not participate in the worship of the Temple, and in this sense they had an heretical character. On the other hand, they carried the cult of observances to a degree of rigor still greater than that of the Pharisees. . . .

CHOURAQUI—That confirms what I said: namely that the Law becomes more important as the bond with the Temple grows weaker. Such was the "Jansenistic" tendency of Judaism. In the measure that you withdraw from the sacrificial life, you are obliged to invent a substitute that will be able to maintain the sociological framework of the religious life. The withdrawal of the Essenes from the sacramental life of the Temple had hardened the importance of the commandments of the Law among them. This is clear, and it is a very important point that deserves to be emphasized.

DANIÉLOU—It is also clear that the Temple of Jerusalem destroyed in 70 has never been rebuilt. It is evident, consequently— you yourself have said it—that the totality of exilic Judaism was established around the question of the observances. It is just this, of course, that has marked it with faith in God. . . .

CHOURAQUI—It was the vehicle, the only vehicle that made the journey possible. . . .

DANIÉLOU—That is so. But it was precisely as a vehicle that the Law appeared to be an essential element for that continuity of which you were just now speaking. To the extent that you stress that it was there as a carapace, a concrete expression constitutive of Judaism as such, you justify in certain respects the position of the apostles and of the first disciples of Christ. In the Old Testament they stressed the elements that appeared to them constitutive —faith in Yahweh, prophecy, and precepts of the moral order, love of one's neighbor—as opposed to the observances that they considered as secondary and not consequently presenting the definitive character offered by the basis of the Law.

You have spoken of the fidelity of Israel, and in particular of its fidelity to the Word of God. It is here that a Christian will find that he is returning to the point that we were discussing a while ago. To a Christian, this fidelity to the Word of God does not seem to imply the pure and simple maintenance of the situation of the ancient period of the history of Israel. It appeared to the apostles that the very fidelity to the Word of God required them to recognize the new elements of the history of God in his people that were represented by the Christian events.

In what you call continuity and in what you call fidelity, there are elements that seem to us completely valid to the same extent that Israel's will to persist in its ethnic characteristics and its own qualities appears well founded. But this fidelity does not seem to us to have the same justification when it consists in maintaining Israel's situation before the events concerning the coming of Jesus, which are decisive for us. The Jews who recognized in Jesus the fulfillment of the prophecies do not seem to us to have been unfaithful to Israel; on the contrary, to our mind they express the very fidelity of Israel. We are always meeting this problem. There are two aspects of Israel that seem to us distinct: that of its persistence as a human community having a right to its own existence, and that of its role in sacred history. Concerning this latter aspect, it is difficult for us to think that Israel always remains the object of an exceptional regime.

To the extent that it seems great and mysterious for Israel at a given time to be the privileged representative of a destiny concerning entire humanity, so all the more does it seem somewhat scandalous that this destiny does not open wide to embrace all men. There is, I am obliged to say, a kind of claim that Israel remains even today the chosen people and that it has a title to a privilege that the other peoples of the earth do not share in the same way. This appears to us wholly unacceptable.

The great thing asked of Israel was that, after being for 2,000 years the only son, it should accept fully in Jesus Christ to be put on the same footing as us, the younger sons and the former pagans, who were called to participate fully in the privileges that up to then were those of Israel alone.

CHOURAQUI—I would like to answer what you have just said by emphasizing that our dialogue is sometimes hindered by clichés that must be challenged. The opposition between Israel and the nations is not the choice of Israel but the result of a definite historical situation. Wishing to save the integrity of the Promise and retiring within itself to preserve the germs of its rebirth, Israel put itself by that fact in a condition to be persecuted. Both of us well remember the events that culminated in the great massacres of the year 1940. May they mark an end forever to a sinister history!

As to the choice, you know that for any doctor worthy of the name it never meant any Jewish racial or ethnic superiority in relation to the rest of the nations. On the contrary, the doctors say that the choice obliged Israel to heavier duties in regard to the other nations. Bahya has written some very fine pages on this. There was never any voluntary disseverance from the nations; there was never in the most authentic Jewish thought—I am not speaking of certain apologetical and polemical writings—a dialectic of opposition between Israel and the nations. On the contrary, all of the great Jewish thinkers hoped that conflicts and contradictions would be bypassed in the march of humanity toward the great messianic unity.

I think the sources attest to what I say. Consult Maimonides who considered Christianity a decisive stage of humanity going toward the messianic reign. Consult Bahya whose thought without any frontiers seems to foretell the great cry of piety and hope of the *Imitation of Christ*. One can indeed say that if there is any ambiguity in the notion of election or choice, we find the identical notion in Christian thought, which is also founded on a choice. I consider what you have just said as entirely true for the exilic period, but it concerns the Church just as much as the Synagogue, the Gentiles as much as the Jews. Now we are witnessing a revolution that constrains us to affirm what we have in common, and to affirm it together in order that together we may ensure its progress. If we wish to preserve the future, we Jews and Christians must keep ourselves forcibly from ready-made ideas inherited from a deplorable past. They are often false and hinder the meeting of hearts and the recognition of souls.

DANIÉLOU—Mr. Chouraqui, you have repeatedly broached the problem of the exilic period and of the condition of the Jews during that time. This is a question that directly concerns Christians, for the period was that of Christian hegemony in the West, and the condition of the Jews was undeniably unhappy. The problem of the responsibility of Christians in this matter was stated by Vatican Council II in its *Declaration on the Relationship of the Church to Non-Christian Religions*.

The reason that clearly causes the Christian conscience of today to tackle this question in a new light is that in modern times anti-Semitism has taken on frightful proportions; we have all been marked by the horrors of the Nazi persecution. On that occasion, Christians had to ask themselves what share of responsibility they may have had in establishing a certain attitude in regard to the Jewish world. These circumstances were the occasion of contacts between Jews and Christians, for if at that time there were frightful persecutions, there were also numerous Christians who discovered a brotherhood with the persecuted Jews. From this there resulted a Judaeo-Christian friendship and all the contacts that led finally to the decisions of Vatican Council II.

This brings us to the problem of anti-Semitism. You yourself said that it is difficult to define a Jew; in the same way, it is not easy to define anti-Semitism. I should like to make a number of remarks, because when one wants to struggle against a reality, one must first state exactly what this reality is. Only in this way can one give a precise point of application to a truly efficacious action.

Here we are no longer in the realm of theories or even of problems concerning the final goals of humanity, however serious these may be. We are concerned with dramatic human problems where it is our duty to do something. There is then one remark I must make. In a few minutes I shall speak of the grave responsibilities of Christians in this matter of anti-Semitism. I believe, however, that it is necessary to note that anti-Semitism is not simply a Christian fact. It existed before Christianity. The bible itself—in the Book of Esther, for example—shows us the persecutions and the pogroms of the Jewish communities by the pagan communities. We know that there was a Greek anti-Semitism, particularly in Alexandria.

To what can this be attributed? I think that this anti-Semitism is the result of what is undeniably the grandeur of Judaism: that is, its inability to be assimilated, to which we have already made allusion. We must define this inability of assimilation. From a cultural point of view, the Jews were very well assimilated. They entered very easily, for example, into the Greek world and very easily into the Latin world. But on account of the particular character of the Jewish religion, the Jews always remained unassimilated in regard to the pagan religions. This is a certain fact. I believe you have stated that they were accused of atheism, as were the Christians at a later date, because they refused to adore the gods of the State. This is indisputably part of their greatness.

Therefore, the Jewish communities appeared as having a particular character, a particular coherence. You yourself remarked that it was a rather extraordinary phenomenon that the Jews survived so many efforts to persecute them and to assimilate them, for there are two ways to suppress a community. One method is simply and purely to destroy it; the other is to assimilate it. Now the Jewish community resisted this twofold effort. I think that here is one of the sources of the anti-Semitism that existed during Christian times. The Jewish communities seemed to be a resistant core. That there were pressures put on them, efforts made to constrain them to conversion, we do not at all deny. But it is equally true that these communities resisted the pressures, and thus they showed themselves to be as unyielding to Christian civilization as they had been to pagan civilization. This is a point of departure that I feel it is important to note.

If we now wish to try to grasp more precisely what was the nature of anti-Semitism during the Christian period—that is, from the time of Constantine to our own day—a few more remarks are in order. I do not think that Christian anti-Semitism developed because the Christians were especially evil. There are some wicked Christians but they certainly are not more wicked than other men. Therefore, we have to look for other reasons that explain why certain hatreds crystallized in regard to the Jewish communities.

The first fact that draws my attention is one to which you have alluded—namely, that the Christian Empire succeeded the Roman Empire. In other words, there was a moment when the political power of the pagan emperors became that of the Christian emperors. It could have become that of Jewish emperors, for there were times between the 1st and the 4th centuries when it was not absolutely certain, as Marcel Simon has so well noted, that the emperors would not be converted to Judaism rather than to Christianity. What Helen succeeded in doing, Berenice had almost accomplished before her. You yourself mentioned how many Jews there were in the entourage of the emperors in the 1st and 2nd centuries and the extent of the Jewish influence at court.

Eventually, however, things turned out differently. It was to Christianity that Constantine and his successors were converted. Christianity became the sociological and official religion of the Empire, just as paganism had been before. From that time the pagans as well as the Jews found themselves on the fringe of the official religion but not necessarily persecuted, although there were some persecutions of the pagans. Nevertheless, both groups were outside the structures of the world in which—and this is something we must never forget—it was unthinkable that one could dissociate totally the political element from the religious. We cannot transpose to the 4th century our conceptions of religious freedom. We must recognize that during that epoch the religious and the political elements formed a kind of bloc; this did not necessarily imply a persecution, but necessarily it did imply a certain segregation. We must recognize this.

It was difficult for it to be otherwise: that is, for the Jews to have in a Christian empire an equality of civil rights with the Christians. There was what we call a ghetto. The great difference between the pagans and the Jews was that the pagans were assimilated. Nothing remains of paganism, except some literary resurrections such as those made in our days by certain men who have rediscovered the ideal of ancient paganism. The pagans were totally assimilated; the Jews were not. We find here that peculiarity, that mystery of Israel which we are discussing. This is, therefore, the first aspect of this period of exile.

Another aspect appears important to me. I think that in the Christian world anti-Semitism was often a popular movement which did not start at the top from the rulers but rather began in local communities. In a rather general manner, the powers—the

religious powers as well as the political, and particularly the
papacy—exercised the role of moderation, assuring Jewish communities a certain number of guarantees and rights. In point of fact,
popular movements led to the atrocious massacres in Germany,
England, France and Italy. These massacres seem connected with
the fact that when there was a crisis, particularly one of material
misery, it was toward the Jews that the fury of the crowds was
directed. This was because the Jews represented a foreign body.
Another reason was that on account of certain of their characteristics in the different domains in which they exercised their activities,
intellectual as well as commercial, they aroused lively jealousy.
The medieval peoples had a kind of anti-Semitic myth that made
the Jew responsible for all evils and all depressions.

I come now to what is more important. Has not Christianity
itself—Christian teaching and the presentation of the events in the
life of Christ as given by Christians—been one of the sources of
anti-Semitism? We are absolutely obliged to say that it has been,
particularly because of the way the events of the life of Christ were
presented, less by the great theologians and the great saints than by
all the popular literature.

CHOURAQUI—Numerous theologians and great saints!

DANIÉLOU—Yes, some. But the problem essentially centers
around the popular presentation of the life of Christ, particularly
in regard to the Passion. The Jews were those who put our Lord to
death, and in the same way that one awakened in the hearts of
children and in the hearts of the Christian people a respect and a
deep love for Jesus Christ, it was almost inevitable that a kind of
fundamental hostility toward the Jews, the wicked Jews, would
develop. I remember singing in my childhood a hymn that said,
"Stop, cruel executioners!" A whole catechetical literature and a
collection of hymns created feelings and a climate favorable to the
development of a really racial anti-Semitism. It is of this that the

contemporary Church has become aware, noting the tragic consequences of this attitude. As you know, this awareness is expressed in an effort to correct what in Christian teaching might be a source of anti-Semitism and to insist first of all. . . .

CHOURAQUI—Before speaking of awareness, I want to go back to what you said about anti-Semitism.

DANIÉLOU—Well, if you wish. . . .

CHOURAQUI—If I spoke of anti-Semitism, it is because I take the condition of the Jews as a whole. It is said that there are three ages of this condition. The first is the biblical age, that of revelation; the second is the exile with its Calvary; the last is when we are assuming the great realities of the return. But I am unable not to live this condition as a whole in which each period explains and throws light on the preceding one. Thus, although it is difficult for me to explain the condition of the Jew, and although the Jew moves along in a paradox, as we said yesterday, one thing is clear: the anti-Semite is defined by his opposition to the Jew. He is one who does not love me inasmuch as I am a Jew.

In the measure that he considers me simply as a Jew, he is opposed to my reality that he despises. It is indeed an absence of love, and consequently an evil. I can speak of Christian anti-Semitism with somewhat more freedom since Jewish blood mingled with Christian blood in the common struggle in which we took part during the Resistance. This alliance of blood resulted in the fruitfulness of the movement of Judaeo-Christian friendship, a movement in which you have been sharing, as I have been, from its very beginnings. There have been Christians who have given their lives for the safety of Jews. I should like to cite only one name, that of Dr. Le Forestier of Le Chambon on the Lignon, who was killed because he openly opposed German anti-Semitism.

Therefore, I believe that it is fitting for me to dispute your analysis by emphasizing certain points.

As a matter of fact, Christian anti-Semitism appears a scandal to me, the more inexplicable since one cannot ignore that it was encouraged and even systematically increased by great theologians and great saints in the Church. One cannot pass over the diatribes of St. John Chrysostom on the Jews against whom he warned the Church. One cannot pass over the Christian anti-Semitic legislation justified by St. Thomas, the Angelic Doctor himself.

Yes, St. Thomas Aquinas, who was not of mediocre intelligence or a writer of catechisms but a man at the summit of intellectual knowledge. You know the famous passage in which St. Thomas Aquinas explained perfectly why the Jews should be segregated; that did not seem to trouble him very much. As you have said, it is not a proof of the special wickedness of Christians to have done that, since this segregation had its roots in the very structure of the medieval State. This was a theocratic state; in order to be a citizen, one had to participate in the intercession of Christ. Now the Jews, faithful to their origins, were not only strangers but strange beings. In Europe they represented a Semitic and an Asiatic presence with their Hebrew characters, their Hebrew books, their phylacteries and their customs inherited from the ancient Semitic East.

All this caused them to be segregated, and in the ghettos they ended up by being regarded as "a type." It can be said that to a certain degree they placed themselves in a position to be persecuted, if one at least admits the fundamental iniquity of the State, for only an iniquitous State could refuse the stranger. Basically their presence in that State was in a negative way what Jesus Christ was in a positive way in the eyes of Christians. They were in truth the unknown brothers of Christ, the people of Jesus, whom the Christians of that epoch could not and would not recognize.

But we have another example of the same kind. I wish to draw your attention to what took place in another theocratic State, the Moslem State. The Jews held there exactly the same role that they held in the Christian State. To have a part in the Christian State, it was necessary to share in the intercession of Christ; to have an integrating part in the Moslem State, it was necessary to share in the intercession of Mahomet. The Jews in both cases were set apart because they did not wish to recognize either Christ or Mahomet. They were on the fringe. It can be said that the legislation of Islam concerning the Jews, codified under the Charter of Omar, resembles very much the codification of the statute of the Jews in Christianity.

However, there are some essential differences which perhaps can help Christians to be aware objectively of their attitude toward the Jews. The first fundamental difference is that the Moslem theologians and jurists recognized and guaranteed the right of the Jews to life and property. This right to life and property was never recognized in regard to the Jews by the canonists in the Christian State. Among the Moslems, the right to property and the rights of the Jews were limited, but it was recognized that the Jews had a certain portion, a certain kind, a certain measure of rights. They were strangers, *dhimmis*, protégés, guests of the Moslem society, admitted on the fringe, but nevertheless definitely admitted. In the medieval Christian city the Jews had no legal existence.

Here is a fundamental difference which should spur the desire of a Christian who wishes to be aware of his past, his history, to see things such as they really were. Do not say that the Jews were strangers only in Europe! In the Moslem state they were also the only strangers. Christianity in the Moslem State was eliminated beginning with the 12th century, and the Jews remained face to face with the Moslems, as they were with the Christians. Now when one considers the history of the Jews in Moslem countries, one sees that their life was quite endurable. The essential contrast with life in Christian countries was that when Islam arose, developed, grew and attained its apogee, it carried the Jews along with it. The fact that the Jews had a particular statute and fulfilled a particular function remained unchanged in the new situation. From the 9th to the 11th century the Jews had almost a monopoly on commerce within the Moslem State. For two centuries they enjoyed an almost exclusive monopoly on the commerce between Europe and Moslem Asia.

Commerce at that time was the source of very great wealth. As a whole series of documents attest, the Jews held the keys to the commerce between Asia, Africa and Europe in the Moslem State. Now these three centuries, the 9th, 10th and 11th, correspond to their intellectual apogee. On the contrary, when Islam was in a state of crisis, fell and entered into a period of decadence beginning with the 14th, 15th and 16th centuries, the Jews followed the same movement. When we analyze the fate of the Jews in Christian lands during the Middle Ages, we perceive that when the nations were in the process of formation, they called upon the Jews; when they were formed, they tolerated them; when they attained their apogee, they drove them away. This difference in fate is general. From the 6th century, we witness expulsions of the Jews in Western Europe. The tendency to persecution persisted until it brought on the fantastic holocaust perpetrated by the Nazis in our generation.

Why this difference between the two theocratic States, one Christian, the other Moslem? For one thing, there is the fact that Christian theocracy was more exclusive, more jealous in its structure, than Moslem theocracy, at least in regard to the Jews. But there is another fact that I think you must admit with sadness, as we have ourselves done. Although the Jews were regarded by the Moslems with a certain contempt, among the Christians this contempt was dominated by a feeling of hatred. To the Moslems the Jew was a *dhimmi,* a protégé. If we consider the Jews as a tribe in the midst of Mohammedan tribes and compare their lot with that of the Mohammedans, we do not note any striking difference. Among the tribes there were tensions, hatreds and wars. Wherever there are men, there are conflicts. When we compare these conflicts, we perceive that the Jews were definitely not more unfortunate than any other tribe of the Moslems. On the contrary, in the 11th century, Bahya said that, all things being taken into account, the poor among the Jews were happier than the little Moslem people, and this in the land of Islam.

Never would any author write a similar thing about the Christian State. There the scorn, nourished against a minority, was transformed into a veritable hatred, such as one vows against the author of the unexpiable crime of deicide. I confess that I have made every possible effort to understand Christian thought, but this monstrous cancer, this accusation of deicide brought against the Jews, I have never succeeded in understanding. I have not succeeded in understanding how it exists among Christians, because it involves two concepts that in my eyes are insane: a collective responsibility and an hereditary responsibility for a crime.

I believe that it is not necessary to be a Christian to understand how much foolishness there is in these two propositions. Tribes who have not given up cannibalism are no longer considered to bear a responsibility that is at the same time collective and hereditary. Even in our own day, certain Christians are still there. Some months ago a Christian whose thought is generally sane—a priest, moreover, although he does not belong to your order—met me and said: "You are of Israel; you are a Jew; you belong to that people who crucified our Lord." The accusation of deicide has ended up being one of those fixed ideas certain Christians have in regard to the Jews.

The *Declaration on the Relationship of the Church to Non-Christian Religions* recently promulgated by Vatican Council II, although it condemns such aberrations, does not innovate anything. Authentic Christian thought cannot admit or support such barbarous and such primitive concepts as those that impute a collective responsibility for any crime whatsoever, much less an hereditary responsibility. Twenty-five centuries and more ago, Ezekiel denounced the concept of collective responsibility and condemned even more forcefully the abracadabra of hereditary responsibility.

No justification or attempt at justification of these tendencies can hold in the face of the reality of the facts. This is all the more true when we remember that the myth of hereditary and collective responsibility has led to a bloody and criminal reality that you indeed know. If I, a Jew, am the author of the greatest crime, the death of God, certainly one should pursue me and kill me. In this domain, at least, the Council has invented nothing, for it only took up the condemnations that date from the Council of Trent, condemnations that have their roots in the bible itself. The innovation

introduced by the Council for the Church consists in really repudi-
ating the errors of the past, putting an end once and for all to the
contradictory concept of Christian anti-Semitism. It will have to
put the texts in operation and make them penetrate into the conscience of each Christian. The Church must discover Israel and
make the sorrow of this people her own and its hope her own.
John XXIII and Paul VI have uttered moving words in this spirit.

DANIÉLOU—I think you have touched upon the root of the
problem in saying that there was something different in the attitude
of the Christians and that of the Moslems. This indeed results from
the fact that the problem of Christ for the Moslems is not the same
as it is for Christians.

The drama comes from the confusion of two orders of questions, and it is precisely this that the Council wished to end. We
have said, and it remains profoundly true, that there is a Judaeo-
Christian confrontation and dialogue on a very high level—the
question of knowing whether or not the events foretold by the
prophets were realized in Jesus Christ. This dialogue remains a
permanent one; the Council did not in any way claim that it would
disappear. It even constitutes one of the highest dialogues of humanity because it shows a preoccupation that absolutely goes beyond any material concerns. I shall say that it is to the honor of
Jews and Christians in the world of today that they assume certain
spiritual values which, although they imply divergences, nevertheless suppose a community of preoccupations.

The drama is that this great problem, which is the very foundation of the Judaeo-Christian dialogue, has interfered with a problem in the sociological order that poisons the theological question
by mingling it with the element of religious passion, the fanaticism
that you mentioned just now in saying that there was hatred among
the Christians but none among the Moslems. This is true. Anti-
Semitism does present one form of fanaticism, that terribly serious
phenomenon appearing throughout the history of humanity, for it
is a deviation of the religious attitude. When the religious attitude
enters into sociological problems, it brings to them a violence that

they do not have of themselves. In this sense, when the religious reality, the highest thing in the world, is set on a plane that is not its own, it brings disturbing elements with it. Fanaticism is something we must detest in all its forms. There are various forms of fanaticism; anti-Semitism is one. This attitude must be definitely and totally denounced. It is this that constitutes the achievement of the Council, for here is a problem that has nothing to do with the religious problem; it is simply a human one.

There is a sociological problem of Judaism; there is a problem of the Jewish people and its place in the world; there is the very special problem posed to the Jewish people by the fact of its dispersion in various countries. On this level there are problems of the same order that you mentioned in regard to Islam: namely, those of the insertion of the Jews into communities where they have not been completely assimilated. Then, finally, there is the great contemporary event, the establishment of the State of Israel that put an end to the dispersion of the Jewish people, a dispersion that was linked to a whole assemblage of historic causes, but which I in no way consider to be the result of a divine curse. Moreover, this dispersion existed long before Christ; the Diaspora has always existed for the Jewish people. In this regard the Jews are a peculiar people. They have always presented this special character of being, on the one hand, a nation, and, on the other hand, dispersed among the nations. This second trait is not at all the expression of a curse. By their commercial genius and their spirit of enterprise, the Jews have always been mingled with all the peoples of the world. . . .

CHOURAQUI—There is no people that has not had its dispersion . . .

DANIÉLOU—Yes, but I believe with the Armenians. . . .

CHOURAQUI—You have a French dispersion. At the present time the Spanish dispersion numbers millions of persons. You have an Italian dispersion, an Irish dispersion, a German dispersion. There is no normal people that does not have its dispersion.

DANIÉLOU—Yes. We are here in the realm of what I shall call sociological problems that in themselves are not likely to arouse any fanaticism, although they may pose real and concrete problems concerning the status of various communities. But these problems, which are positive and concern the temporal destiny of the Jewish people, interfere with another order of problems which are also real but which should not interfere with them: namely, those which concern Israel's place in the history of salvation and its relations with Christianity.

Here we touch upon a very important point in our dialogue. It is essential today that the two problems should be dissociated. The commitment of the Council is a very profound commitment. You were saying just now that it is not a question of remaining on the level of words. But, for my part, I am absolutely convinced, through the contacts I had with the bishops during the Council, that it is not at all a question of words. The will of all the bishops of the world was to put a definite end to all that is responsible for the Christian roots of anti-Semitism.

From this point of view, the attitude of the Church is absolutely decided. But at the same time it is very important for the Jews to understand that the Church cannot touch what is the very expression of her message: that is, anything that concerns the person of Christ and the relation between the Old and the New Testaments.

You have made allusions to several questions; on these questions it is important that we explain ourselves very clearly. One thing has been established that is of great moment for Christian teaching, and it has been favored by the biblical movement among Christians: namely that all Christians should perpetually bear in mind the eminent dignity of the Jewish people among all peoples. There is a privilege of the Jewish people that is inalienable—to have been the chosen people.

From this people have come the Virgin Mary, the apostles,

Peter the first pope and Jesus according to the flesh. This should develop a very special respect in young Christians for a people from whom came forth the representatives of the foundations of their faith. Likewise there are certain side issues about which I have often spoken with Jules Isaac. We must not present the Judaism of the time of Christ as being in complete decadence. We must not make an absurd criticism of Pharisaism. On the contrary, we know that the Pharisees were deeply religious men. . . .

CHOURAQUI—Of whom the Church is the direct heir. St. Paul was a Pharisee, and the essential theme of the Pharisees' doctrines has informed the dogma of the Church. . . .

DANIÉLOU—We must not either, as we have already said, make the dispersion a consequence of the crucifixion! There is a whole mass of accepted ideas that you previously called ready-made schematizations. They exist in some minds and used to be found in manuals. Today they must definitely be liquidated.

In addition to these, other fundamental problems present themselves. Christians cannot help considering that there is a relation of continuity between what we call the Old and the New Testaments. From this point of view, the problem of placing the present-day Jewish people in the Christian vision presents a real difficulty. It is impossible for a Christian not to consider that Christ is really the eschatological event foretold by the prophets, the one who fully realized in himself all the messianic hopes.

In this perspective, the Jews who followed Jesus were conscious of being the authentic continuers of the people of ancient Israel. For us, sacred history continues today. What was at first the privilege of Israel alone is today open to all nations, and in this sense it is not possible for us to see in contemporary Israel the people of God in the way that Israel was the people of God before Christ. For us, the people of God has extended today in the Church to all nations. There is a continuity of Israel that a Christian fully accepts—that of Israel constituting a particular human type, a human type that has an absolute right to exist and to persist in existence. This people has the right to have a country, the right to be a people among other peoples. But in what I would call sacred history, salvation history, this people can no longer be for us today what it was in the Old Testament.

In this sense, there is something that we cannot give up because it is precisely our mission: that is, to announce Jesus Christ to every man, as St. Paul said, whether he be pagan or Jew. We recognize perfectly—and this is the meaning of the text on religious freedom—that every man must act according to his conscience and that constraint of any kind whatever must be definitely rejected. But that does not mean that we can regard the religious situation of Israel to be on the same level as the religious situation of Christians. This should be evident from the fact of the significance of Christ for Christians.

But I insist on emphasizing it, for I have heard eminent Jewish personalities say: "We shall understand one another the day you give up trying to convert us." This is an expression that we cannot accept. We cannot give up trying to convert you. We can respect you profoundly in your sincerity and your religious values; we can fully recognize your right to exist as a people; we can condemn all that comes from any pressure whatever to convert you. But there is something I cannot do. I am unable *not* to say to you who sit beside me that in Jesus Christ the event foretold by the prophets has come, as St. Peter told your ancestors on the day after Pentecost.

Finally, I add a last point. What I have just said is very important, for it would be serious if there were any ambiguity about it. It would be serious if you would reproach us for not conceding to you points that we cannot concede. The concessions would be a betrayal of ourselves; more exactly (for it is not a question of betraying oneself), they would be a betrayal of a truth of which we have no right to dispose. The other day, in an article in *Le Monde,* Monsieur Garaudy stated his belief that the Council had done a marvelous thing inasmuch as henceforth the Church would accept what is called pluralism. This pluralism would mean that the fact of being a Jew, the fact of being a Communist, the fact of being a Christian, the fact of being a Buddhist, would appear as so many free choices, each one choosing what he liked.

Now this would be in direct contradiction to what we have to bear witness to together: that is, a belief in the existence of truth, even if we disagree on what this truth is. In order to bear positive fruits and to establish a common action, our dialogue must first of all imply that we accept one another as we are and that we do not reproach one another for not saying pleasant things that do not correspond to our thought. It is not a question of being pleasant; it is a question of being first of all true. A true dialogue, a true collaboration can be founded only on this.

CHOURAQUI—Now we are warned. As for me, I am grateful to you for having said these things with so much frankness. I believe indeed that it is by frankness that we shall succeed in rediscovering one another, in recognizing one another. You spoke of conversion. The sensibility of Jews is irritated by converters, mainly because of the conversion of some souls precious in the eyes of a minority that is at times obliged to defend itself at the price of its blood in order to survive.

The Jews of the Diaspora were on the defensive, especially in Christian countries. They had the feeling that to persevere in existence was for them, in the harsh realities of exile, the surest way to share in the final goals of humanity. To remain a Jew became an end in itself; it was something essential for them and for humanity. You know what persecutions they had to face simply to persevere in existence.

When converters appeared, the difficulties in persevering increased. But when these converters used underhanded, even blamable means, it must be said that their action was intolerable. Intolerable were the stakes lighted to save souls; intolerable were the petty and unworthy means very often used by certain missions whose methods are repudiated by the Church herself. Intolerable also were certain proceedings that would be out of place even in the most remote and backward parts of the world and which are completely inefficacious, if not harmful, in a country like Israel where the most insignificant ten-year-old child knows as much of the bible as many experienced theologians. I do not believe I am betraying the truth in saying that. The means used by the missions must be rigorously chosen.

I often defend your point of view against Christians who claim that they do not wish to convert us. To these Christians (I often say the same thing to my Jewish friends who revolt against the ways of the missions), I answer that when the Christians stop wanting to convert us, it is then that I shall become an anti-Christian! Since the Church aspires to convert the entire universe, why do you expect that she will discriminate against us and that she will renounce us? Thus I believe that your frankness is good. Nevertheless, we must understand one another on the meaning of the word "conversion."

We can conclude this debate, I believe, by trying to define the meaning and the means of the mission, the mission that we must all fulfill. Fundamentally the idea of mission is a Jewish one. The first missionaries of the world were Jews, and they shared the extraordinary destiny of seeing their national religion become a universal one with only one other people, the Arabs. Outside these two missionary peoples, all of humanity has been proselytized.

Is not the true mission definitely that of bringing about the order of justice and love? Instead of trying to convert one another, should we not try together to convert ourselves to what we preach? Are not the best missionaries those who renounce acting upon others in order to act upon themselves and to enlighten the world by example? It is this that the Church must be taught again. You should perhaps be grateful to the Jews for their constant opposition to the preaching of the proselytizers. At least they recalled the reality that one can definitely convert only oneself. And judging by my personal experience, one has enough trouble doing this for oneself.

The only possible radiation of a religion is the example it

gives—its works, its fruits. You were speaking of pluralism. Permit me to quote what was said by one who for me always remains a true Jew: Jesus. "In my father's house there are many mansions." Although one must not interpret the decisions of the Council as an incitement to syncretism where thought and its exigencies would disappear or be downgraded, I believe that they could be interpreted as asking men to be at least as tolerant as God.

God admits plurality of mansions in his dwelling; he admits that "the just" and "the wicked" dwell together. The command that Jesus, following Moses, gives to us is: "You shall love the Lord your God with your whole heart." Nearly everyone interprets this command to mean: "You shall love *the idea that you have of* the Lord your God with your whole heart." It is here that the separation takes place. We interpose our limited psychological conceptions between creation and the infinite love of God. I believe that we must above all return to the sources of Love and know that our thoughts are feeble before infinite Light and the infinite Love of the Uncreated. I believe that in this requirement, which is a requirement of pure thought, we can admit a certain pluralism which would not be the cause of any deadening or diminishing of conceptual and dogmatic differences, but rather a real incitement toward the final goals of humanity, toward the realization of the supreme order of unity and love that is common to Jews and Christians.

DANIÉLOU—What you have said—that for each one conversion is first the conversion of himself—is profoundly true. What each one must struggle to do is to convert himself to more justice and more love. This conversion is the primary task.

However, we must not minimize the question of truth. You yourself recalled that the Jews were the first missionaries and that they rendered witness to the living God in the face of an idolatrous world. They certainly did not put the God who had manifested himself to them on the same footing with the pagan divinities, although they respected pagan values. In like manner, a Christian must bear witness to the truth of which he is the depositary. He desires to see it shared by others. I do not say he should impose his truth on others, but simply that he should testify to the truth while desiring to see it shared by others.

CHOURAQUI—I should like to respond to what has dominated your thought and words since the beginning of this dialogue and to add some words on the person of Christ. Through the course of the centuries, the Jews have not encountered Christ, and what they knew of Christians was unfortunately not always the best. This is evident, I believe, in the first three centuries of the Church. There was little contact between Christian thought and Jewish thought and the impact of Christianity on the Jewish people as a whole was very weak. In these beginnings, only minorities were touched by Christian thought. The Jews did not then regard Christian missionaries as strangers to their people, but only as representatives of one of the numberless sects that abounded at that time.

When the Church identified herself or had a tendency to identify herself with the Empire, the conflict in some way became national. The Jew had to preserve himself against the Empire, the enemy of Israel. There was a constant merging of the two realities: the Church on the one hand, the Empire on the other. And that naturally made a screen between the Jews and the person and teachings of Jesus. When the Christians and the Jews fought to impose their spiritual supremacy over the Empire, the veil became more impenetrable.

The turning that the Church took beginning with the 4th century, the anti-Semitic legislation that she promulgated, the crime of Judaism that she tracked down—all these facts permitted other very real crimes to be committed against the Jews. The gap widened and became an abyss. When we examine Jewish literature from the 5th to the 19th century, we perceive that if at times there were some Judaeo-Christian polemics, they were rare and remained on the lowest level of invective between groups that confronted and fought one another without taking into account historic truth and the exigencies of pure thought. Certainly the Judaeo-Christian conflict increased the distance between the Jews and a calm knowledge of Christian thought, just as it hid the depths of Israel from the Church.

The result was that the average Jew came to identify the Christian with the anti-Semite. I have thus known well-meaning young Jews to consider Jesus not as he really was but as the leader of a social group whose vocation, whose mission, was to desire and organize the extermination of the Jews. It is necessary to say these things because they exist. And since the Jews in Europe have undergone the fate of which we are all well aware, how can we ask them to make a clear distinction between Christian peoples (besides who would they be?) and peoples that have been Christianized, or between the concepts of Christianity and those of the Church?

There was an almost inevitable identification, and although I am opposed to the concept of collective responsibility, I cannot say that the ideas of which we have just spoken are absolutely independent. That a Germany which had been Christianized, really Christianized, since the beginnings of the Christian era could have committed crimes such as those perpetrated in our generation truly implies a certain responsibility and a certain interference of one domain in another, of the spiritual in the temporal. Who could deny this?

You tell me—and I am inclined to hope for it, to believe it, to think it—that Christianity is turning away from those errors that may be called criminal, that have led to so many tears, so much bloodshed, so much unjustified hatred. But if there was a debate, a theological conflict, between Jews and Christians, was that a sufficient reason to make the Jews undergo the treatment they have undergone, to drag them into the horror and mud of so many massacres?

If then we can turn the page, with all of us trying to efface the aftermath of the past, the hope of a twofold discovery springs up. The first discovery will be, allow me to say, that the Church will recognize her Hebrew roots. Nobody can recognize better than yourself the importance, in some way ontological, of this new graft. Beginning with the 4th century, when the Church withdrew from the Jews, she withdrew also from her Hebrew roots. Now the tree of Israel, as St. Paul said, bears the Church that is the grafted olive tree. The revival of the roots, the true Judaeo-Christian reconciliation, will perhaps permit what St. Paul compares to the resurrection of the dead. This mystic forecast has come much closer to realization in our days.

I see already—the State of Israel is only eighteen years old—the extraordinary importance that the Hebrew rebirth there has for the Church. The Christians living in Israel have suddenly rediscovered the bible in Hebrew; they have rediscovered the literature contemporary with Christ and the literature anterior to him, the immense current of Hebrew literature, the Talmudic literature that is a constant meditation on the bible at the summit of the highest thought, on the bible that is yours as well as ours.

This rediscovery is for me the harbinger of the revival of the roots. For the Church there is a turning point that foretells for her a real metamorphosis on the threshold of a new era. Christianity in its entirety will be revivified by biblical knowledge. You made an allusion to the biblical renewal. Allow me to remark that this renewal is exactly contemporaneous with the renewal of Hebrew, and also contemporaneous with the rebirth of Jerusalem. These are two parallel movements that are not without influence on each other.

Now one thing becomes more and more clear. This renaissance concerns not only the Jews, not only the Catholic Church, but entire humanity in its march toward the realization of its unity. It is at the source that one is reunited. Thus the meeting of Paul VI and Athenagoras could not have had another site than that of Jerusalem. This Jerusalem now speaks Hebrew, biblical Hebrew, the language of David and of Ezekiel.

To the degree that the Church rediscovers her Hebrew sources, she will work for her unity, and she will also work for the unity of the world in drawing near to that East which today contains two-thirds of the human race. Let me note that you Christians and we Jews are only a small minority of humanity—a very small minority —and although we are important, we are not alone. Two-thirds of humanity is waiting to drink at that spring which appears to us so salutary and so redeeming.

When we consider the reality of this two-thirds of the human race, our rivalries, our disputes, our rancors, the more or less bittersweet memories that we can evoke, our differences—all become dim. We can then become aware of what brings us together and makes us one. Our fidelities and our betrayals accuse us with the same finger, do they not?

Now in what concerns the position of the Jews regarding Christ, I have said there has been not so much a meeting as a conflict. When a meeting took place, it often happened that the Jew became a Christian and ceased to be a Jew. At the present time we are living in the age of the return, and, as you said, it is possible that there are Jews who are of the Christian confession. Such, indeed, is the case in Israel.

But there is more. The new world in which we live and the evolution of the deepest tendencies of Christian thought have likewise transformed the Jewish attitude toward Christ. You have cited the names of Edmond Fleg, Jules Isaac and Shalom Ash. One could cite many others, and notably two great men who in the name of Israel have admitted the Christian act in all its reality, in all its objectivity, and also in all its grandeur. These men to whom I refer are Rosenzweig and Martin Buber.

The thought of Martin Buber is known in France; that of Rosenzweig is unfortunately not enough known. This man, who died in Germany in 1929 at the age of forty-three, discovered Judaism through Christianity. Such was also true in the case of numerous Western Jews. Rosenzweig's masterpiece, *The Star of Redemption,* written in 1921, establishes Judaism no longer as a doctrinal teaching but as a category of being. The Jewish existence constitutes an ontological event that establishes and allows us to refind the real significance of the universal and the human. For Rosenzweig the revelation made to Israel orientates all humanity toward the future of the kingdom of God that it prefigures, and it succeeds in giving each creature the possibility of saying "we" that constitutes for the "I" the saving act of saying "thou" to a "he."

Christianity, whose divine mission consists in making the pagan world enter the kingdom of God, and Judaism both incarnate here below a category of life eternal, and both lead to the eternity of time. The Church, whose way extends between the coming of Christ and his return, is situated, according to Rosenzweig, above history, and yet she must fulfill all history. The world is transparent for her. Thus Israel has eternity sealed in its very nature; it is the transhistoric effulgence that is in the eternal present of creation, of revelation, of redemption. That is why it is ever necessary for the verification of Christian truth. The continuance of Jewish interiority thus constitutes the supreme action of Israel in the progress of the ecumenism of the Church and of Christ.

A global awareness of the Judaeo-Christian phenomenon would permit an immense historic advance and mark a decisive step toward the accomplishment of human unity. In order to hasten the fulfillment of this unity, it would be necessary to put an end not only to the absurdity of Christian anti-Semitism, but also to missionary practices that are unworthy both of the Church and of Israel. We should begin by ceasing to dispute and trying to inform one another as completely as possible. We have not as yet begun to work in this direction.

At the present time, the Jews have said "yes" to a country, to a culture, to a language, to a land; in addition they have been forced to say "yes" to the nations and to meet the Churches. In this change of attitude there is certainly not a solution of all our conflicts, but there is a new possibility of dialogue, of reciprocal enrichment and, even more, of a new dynamism, in supporting ourselves by our mutual help in order to advance together toward the goals that are common to us.

DANIÉLOU—I believe you have expressed things very well in saying that what is now essential is this encounter. It is astonishing to think that today, for example, there is an excellent specialist in the New Testament at the Hebrew university of Jerusalem, and that rabbinical studies are flourishing in Christian lands. On the level of this objective information, the first element for a reciprocal understanding and knowledge, there is thus a great advance on both sides.

In ending, I should like to stress, as you yourself said, that in addition to this effort at mutual understanding and dialogue, there is the possibility of a work in common.

Although there are opposing views—we have admitted this and we must not minimize the fact—there is also a common heritage, the bible, which expresses itself through the Jewish law and which was taken up by Christ in formulas from the Old Testament. When Christ said: "Thou shalt love the Lord thy God with thy whole heart, and with thy whole soul, and with thy whole strength, and with thy whole mind, and thy neighbor as thyself," he was taking two formulas, one from Leviticus and the other from Deuteronomy. This formula that appears to be the very synthesis of the Christian ideal was already a Jewish formula. We feel today how necessary it is for us to draw near one another in order to accomplish the tasks that are common to us.

A short time ago you evoked the word "justice." This is a word of great importance to me, for it has kept clear in my mind the meaning of the Hebrew *tsedek,* a word that has another and infinitely deeper significance than what men around us all too often call justice. We know that the problem of present-day civilization goes beyond that of a just sharing of material goods. Certainly justice includes this sharing, but far beyond that, it is also the conformity of civilization to the designs of God. This effort to create not only a world in which men may be happier materially, but also one that is more conformable to the dignity of man—that we have in common. I shall add that it is common not only to us but also in large part to our Moslem brothers.

This Mediterranean world has been tragically divided in the course of the centuries, and these divisions have perhaps hindered it from bearing the testimony it should have borne. If it is capable today of surmounting these divisions, there is a possibility of finding again a certain brotherhood, of bringing to the world a message that is precisely what the world awaits. You were saying a moment ago that certain quarrels seem inadmissible in the face of certain dramas in the world of today, and that when there is something to be built, we have no longer the right to lose ourselves in vain fratricidal struggles.

This expresses what we think together. We are both working at this task in proportion to our strength. In order to put the stress today on what we have in common—on our common heritage, on that vision of human destiny, on faith in a God of love—we must liquidate a number of dramas which have been tragic and into which we must never fall again.

CHOURAQUI—We are in truth the heirs of the same great tradition, and we are united even by that which divides us. To the degree that the turmoil of our quarrels will die down, we shall become more aware of the roots that bear and nourish us. First of all, the bible, of which you have spoken with so much eloquence, remains the rock on which our dwellings are built. The biblical tradition is also common to us. Christianity must strive to discover what it was and what it has become in Judaism, while the Jews, as certain ones have already done in Israel, must become aware of the deep "Judaicity" of the Church whose thought will have to be retranslated and reinterpreted in Hebrew.

On the summit, the encounter is easy, is it not? Bahya ibn Paquda and St. Bonaventure, for example, both employ the same seraphic language; they are both dialecticians, poets and mystics, visibly inspired by the same vision, by the same thirst, by the same hunger for the absolute.

We must also discover that our liturgies, both Christian and Jewish, have the psalms, the great inspirations and the great aspirations, as well as the intellecutal structures. Instead of persisting in fighting about what still divides us, let us become aware of the immense and marvelous realities that make us brothers. Gregorian music is the heir and continuation of the music of the Temple. The chalice you use at Mass, even down to the detail of the widening of its base, is the exact replica of the chalice that the high priest used to raise in the Hebrew liturgy of the Temple. The great Rabbi Toledano, who was Primate of Zion and Minister of Religions, told me that only a Talmudist could understand at its true depth the liturgy of the Christian Mass. Yes, we have immense treasures to rediscover together, sources of inspiration which we can truly place at the service of all humanity. But our reconciliation will remain imperfect as long as it does not extend to Ishmael, who is, as you have stressed, also an heir of Abraham.

The Mediterranean is peopled on its south shores by Moslems, on its east shores by Jews, and on its northern shores by Christians. Therefore, the reconciliation of the children of Abraham could bring about the formation of a new entity, composed of peoples who are inspired by the same heritage and who aspire to the triumph of the same biblical values—spiritual, moral and social.

The Mediterranean unity of which you dream and for which we must all work could in our day express in political terms the promise made to Abraham 4,000 years ago and effect its realization for the salvation of the world. The nations of the world could thus be really blessed by the reconciliation of Abraham's posterity and fraternally associated to ensure the triumph of peace over war, of love over hatred, of light over darkness.

The reconciliation of Jews, Christians and Moslems would condition in our time the assembling of spiritual, moral, political and social forces, the concentration of which could form an obstacle to atomic warfare, to hunger and to ignorance, and their union would not only serve but perhaps save the human race. On our choice may depend whether the order of unity and of love, dreamed of by the prophets and foretold by the apostles, will become in our day the new order of a humanity that has been pacified, reconciled and saved.

Statement of Vatican Council II on the Jews [1]

As the Council searches into the mystery of the Church, it remembers the spiritual bonds which tie the people of the New Covenant to the offspring of Abraham.

Thus the Church of Christ acknowledges that, according to God's saving mystery, the beginnings of her faith and her election are found already in the patriarchs, Moses and the prophets. She professes that all who believe in Christ—Abraham's sons according to the faith (cf. Gal. 3, 7)—are included in this patriarch's call, and likewise that the salvation of the Church is symbolically prefigured in the exodus of the chosen people from the land of bondage. The Church, therefore, cannot forget that she received the revelation of the Old Testament through the people with whom God in his inexpressible mercy made the ancient covenant. Nor can she forget that she draws sustenance from the root of that well-cultivated olive tree onto which have been grafted the wild shoots, the Gentiles (cf. Rom. 11, 17-24). Indeed, the Church believes that by his cross Christ, who is our Peace, reconciled Jews and Gentiles, making the two one in himself (cf. Eph. 2, 14-16).

The Church keeps ever in mind the words of the Apostle about his kinsmen: "Theirs is the sonship and the glory and the covenant and the law and the worship and the promises; theirs are the fathers and from them is the Christ according to the flesh" (Rom. 9, 4-5), the Son of the Virgin Mary. She also recalls that the apostles, the Church's foundation stones and pillars, as well as most of the early disciples who proclaimed the Gospel of Christ to the world, sprang from the Jewish people.

As holy scripture testifies, Jerusalem did not recognize the time of her visitation (cf. Lk. 19, 44), nor did the Jews, in large number, accept the Gospel; indeed, not a few of them opposed its

[1] The following statement, printed in its entirety, is taken from the *Declaration on the Relation of the Church to Non-Christian Religions*, n. 4 (Glen Rock N.J.: Paulist Press, 1966), pp. 12-14.

dissemination (cf. Rom. 11, 28). Nevertheless, now as before, God holds the Jews most dear for the sake of their fathers; he does not repent of the gifts he makes or of the calls he issues—such is the witness of the Apostle (cf. Rom. 11, 28-29; also cf. *Dogmatic Constitution on the Church: A.A.S.* 57 [1965], p. 20). In company with the prophets and the same Apostle, the Church awaits that day, known to God alone, on which all peoples will address the Lord with a single voice and "serve him with one accord" (Soph. 3, 9: cf. Is. 66, 23; Ps. 65, 4; Rom. 11, 11-32).

Since the spiritual patrimony common to Christians and Jews is then so rich, the Council wishes to foster and commend mutual understanding and esteem. This will be the fruit, above all, of biblical and theological studies and of brotherly dialogues.

True, the Jewish authorities and those who followed their lead pressed for the death of Christ (cf. Jn. 19, 6); still, what happened in his passion cannot be charged against all the Jews, without distinction, then alive, nor against the Jews of today. Although the Church is the new People of God, the Jews should not be represented as rejected by God or accursed, as if this followed from holy scripture. All should see to it, then, that in catechetical work and in the preaching of the Word of God they teach nothing save what conforms to the truth of the Gospel and the spirit of Christ.

The Church, moreover, rejects every persecution against any man. For this reason and for the sake of the patrimony she shares with the Jews, the Church decries hatreds, persecutions and manifestations of anti-Semitism directed against Jews at any time and by anyone. She does so, not impelled by political reasons, but moved by the spiritual love of the Gospel.

Besides, Christ underwent his passion and death freely and out of infinite love because of the sins of men in order that all might reach salvation. This the Church has always taught and teaches still; it is therefore the duty of the Church to proclaim the cross of Christ as the sign of God's all-embracing love and as the fountain from which every grace flows.

Bibliographical Note

In the course of the last few years, the French language has been enriched by texts and studies on Israel, its history, tradition, structures and problems. For the reader who is eager to deepen his knowledge, we indicate the two principal collections: "Sinaï," published by the Presses Universitaires de France, and "Présence du Judaisme," published by Albin Michel. They include works that should be read, notably the monumental *Histoire d'Israël* by S. W. Baron. (Collection "Sinaï," P.U.F.)

The works of Edmond Fleg (*Anthologie juive, Ecoute Israel . . .*), Jules Isaac (*Jésus et Israël*), Georges Vajda (*L'Amour de Dieu dans la Théologie juive du Moyen Age*) and André Neher (*Le Puits de l'Exil*) belong to a movement that tends to reintegrate Jewish thought into the intellectual horizons of the West.

Poets (André Spire, Claude Vigée, Joseph Milbauer, Emmanuel Eydoux), historians (Léon Poliakov, Robert Aron, C. Gruber-Magittot), novelists (Albert Cohen, Manès Sperber, Elie Wiesel, André Schwartzbart, Albert Memmi, Arnold Mandel, Anna Langfus) and essayists (Nicholas Baudy, Josué Jéhouda, Robert Misrahi, André Chouraqui, Henri Serouya) reexamine the Jewish problem under the most diverse aspects, while philosophers (Emmanuel Levinas, Eliane Amado-Levy-Valensi) go back courageously to the sources of Israel's thought. Let us cite also the great works of Raymond Aron, Henri Baruk, Robert Brunschwig, René Cassin, Georges Friedmann, Vladimir Jankélevitch, Pierre-Maxime Schuhl, Jean Wahl and Eric Weil. Although they do not all belong to Jewish thought, nevertheless they give back to it the light it has given them.

Following the trend of thought that Pascal and Bossuet made illustrious, Christians consider the mystery of Israel. Léon Bloy, Charles Péguy, Paul Claudel, Jean Daniélou, Jean de Menasce (*Quand Israël aime Dieu*), Paul Vuillaud, Jacques Madaule, Claude Tresmontant, Marcel Simon, Edouard Dhorme and Dupont-Sommer have contributed to the establishment in France of a center where the thought of Israel, leaving its exile, is revivified in the movements of our times.

Finally Jacques Maritain, in his very fine book *Le Mystère d'Israel et autres essais* (Desclée de Brouwer: Paris, 1965), gathers together and completes the scattered pages on which in the course of his life he has treated of Israel's destiny. This work reports the history of the struggle that led to the decisions of Vatican Council II in regard to the Jews, as well as the historic revision, now being accomplished, of the relations between Jews and Christians.

Bibliography

I

WORKS BY JEAN DANIÉLOU

Biblical Studies

The Presence of God. Mowbrays, 1958.
The Bible and Liturgy. University of Notre Dame, 1956.
From Shadows to Reality. Newman, 1960.
Holy Pagans of the Old Testament. Helicon, 1957.
In the Beginning—Genesis. Helicon, 1965.
The Work of John the Baptist. Helicon, 1966.

Judaeo-Christianity

The Theology of Judaeo-Christianity. Regnery, 1964.
Symbols of the Primitive Church. Helicon, 1964.
A New History of the Catholic Church. vol. I. McGraw Hill, 1964.
Etudes d'Exégèse Judéo-Chrétienne. Paris, 1966.

Studies on Judaism

Philon d'Alexandre. Paris, 1958.
Dialogue avec Israel. Paris, 1963.

Theology of History

The Salvation of the Nations. University of Notre Dame, 1962.
The Advent of Salvation. Paulist Press.
Lord of History. Regnery, 1958.

II

WORKS BY ANDRÉ CHOURAQUI

Juridical Studies

La Création de l'Etat d'Israël, thesis for the Doctorate in Law, Paris, 1948.

The Social and Legal Status of the Jews of French Morocco, preface by Jacob Blaustein, New York, 1953.

History and Sociology

Les Juifs d'Afrique du Nord. Paris, 1952. Work crowned by the Zadoc Kahn Foundation.

History of Judaism. Walker, 1963.

L'Etat d'Israel. Paris, 1956.

L'Alliance Israélite Universelle et la Renaissance Juive Contemporaine, preface by René Cassin, Presses Universitaires de France, Paris, 1965.

Biblical Studies

Les Psaumes. Paris, 1956.

Le Cantique des Cantiques. Paris, 1952.

Introduction aux Livres Sapientiaux de la Bible. Bible oecumenique, Editions Planète, 1965.

Medieval Philosophy

Introduction aux Devoirs des Coeurs de Bahya Ibn Paquda, preface by Jacques Maritain, Paris, 1950.

La Couronne du Royaume de Salomon Ibn Gabirol. Revue thomiste, Paris, 1952.

Biography

Theodore Herzl, Editions du Seuil, Paris, 1960. Chosen by the Club des Editeurs, Paris, 1960.

Essays

La Pensée Juive. Presses Universitaires de France, 1965.
Les Racines qui nous portent (To be published by Mame).

Poetry

Cantique pour Nathanael. Corti, Paris, 1960.

Supplementary Reading

Baron, S. W. *A Social and Religious History of the Jews.* 8 vol. Columbia University Press, 1957.

Baum, Gregory. *Is the New Testament Anti-Semitic?* Paulist Press Deus Book, 1965.

Berdyaev, Nicolas. *Christianity and Anti-Semitism.* Philosophical Library, 1954.

Bevan, E. R., ed. *The Legacy of Israel.* Clarendon, 1927.

Buck, H. M. *People of the Lord.* Macmillan, 1966.

Daniel-Rops, H. *Israel and the Ancient World.* Eyre and Spottiswood, 1949.

Démann, Paul. *Judaism. Twentieth Century Encyclopedia of Catholicism.* vol. 73 Hawthorne, 1961.

Elbogen, Ismar. *A Century of Jewish Life.* Jewish Publication Society of America, 1960.

Epstein, Isidore. *Judaism.* Penguin, 1964.

Fleg, Edmond. *The Jewish Anthology.* Behrman, 1940.

Gelin, Albert. *The Religion of Israel. Twentieth Century Encyclopedia of Catholicism.* vol. 65, Hawthorne, 1959.

Gordon, Cyrus. *The World of the Old Testament.* Doubleday, 1958.

Glatzer, N. N. *Franz Rosenzweig: His Life and Thought.* Schocken.

Graetz, Heinrich. *History of the Jews.* 6 vol. J.P.S.A., 1956.

Grayzel, Solomon. *A History of the Jews.* J.P.S.A., 1963.

Isaac, Jules. *The Teaching of Contempt: Christian Roots of Anti-Semitism.* Holt, Rinehart and Winston, 1964.

Kennedy, J. K. *On Israel, Zionism, and the Jewish Issue.* Herzl Press, 1965.

Margolis, H. L. and Marx, Alexander. *A History of the Jewish People.* J.P.S.A., 1961.

Maritain, Jacques. "The Mystery of Israel," *Redeeming the Time.* Chapter VI. Bles, 1944.

Maritain, Jacques. *A Christian Looks at the Jewish Question.* Longmans, 1939.

Moore, G. F. *Judaism*. 3 vol. Harvard University Press, 1962.

Osterreicher, J. M., ed. *The Bridge*. 4 vol. Yearbook of Judaeo-Christian Studies. Pantheon, 1955-1962.

Roth, Cecil. *History of the Jews*. Schocken. 1964.

Sachar, H. M. *The Course of Modern Jewish History*. World, 1958.

Scholem, G. G. *Major Trends in Jewish Mysticism*. Schocken. 1956.

Schwarz. L. W., ed. *Great Ages and Ideas of the Jewish People*. Modern Library, 1956.

Sklare, Marshall, ed. *The Jews and the Social Patterns of an American Group*. Free Press, 1960.

Tresmontant, Claude. *A Study of Hebrew Thought*. Desclee de Brouwer, 1960.

Vaux, Roland de. *Ancient Israel*. McGraw, 1961.